Avoiding the Corporate Death Spiral

Also available from ASQ Quality Press:

The Certified Manager of Quality/Organizational Excellence Handbook, Third Edition
Russell T. Westcott, editor

Transformational Leadership: Creating Organizations of Meaning
Stephen Hacker and Tammy Roberts

Managing with Conscience for Competitive Advantage
Pete Geissler

Everyday Excellence: Creating a Better Workplace through Attitude, Action, and Appreciation
Clive Shearer

Making Change Work: Practical Tools for Overcoming Human Resistance to Change
Brien Palmer

Business Performance through Lean Six Sigma: Linking the Knowledge Worker, the Twelve Pillars, and Baldrige
James T. Schutta

Leadership For Results: Removing Barriers to Success for People, Projects, and Processes
Tom Barker

Inside Knowledge: Rediscovering the Source of Performance Improvement
David Fearon and Steven A. Cavaleri

The Six Sigma Path to Leadership: Observations from the Trenches
David H. Treichler

The Executive Guide to Improvement and Change
G. Dennis Beecroft, Grace L. Duffy, and John W. Moran

To request a complimentary catalog of ASQ Quality Press publications, call 800-248-1946, or visit our website at http://qualitypress.asq.org.

Avoiding the Corporate Death Spiral

Recognizing and Eliminating the Signs of Decline

Gregg Stocker

ASQ Quality Press
Milwaukee, Wisconsin

American Society for Quality, Quality Press, Milwaukee 53203
© 2006 Gregg Stocker
All rights reserved. Published 2006
Printed in the United States of America

12 11 10 09   5 4 3 2

Library of Congress Cataloging-in-Publication Data
Stocker, Gregg, 1959–
  Avoiding the corporate death spiral : recognizing and eliminating the signs of decline / Gregg Stocker.
    p. cm.
  Includes bibliographical references and index.
  ISBN 0-87389-684-X (pbk. : alk. paper)
  1. Organizational effectiveness.   2. Management.   3. Business failures.
  I. Title.

HD58.9.S755 2006
658.4′063—dc22   2006001952

ISBN-10: 0-87389-684-X
ISBN-13: 978-0-87389-684-9

No part of this book may be reproduced in any form or by any means, electronic, mechanical, photocopying, recording, or otherwise, without the prior written permission of the publisher.

Publisher: William A. Tony
Acquisitions Editor: Annemieke Hytinen
Project Editor: Paul O'Mara
Production Administrator: Randall Benson

ASQ Mission: The American Society for Quality advances individual, organizational, and community excellence worldwide through learning, quality improvement, and knowledge exchange.

Attention Bookstores, Wholesalers, Schools, and Corporations: ASQ Quality Press books, videotapes, audiotapes, and software are available at quantity discounts with bulk purchases for business, educational, or instructional use. For information, please contact ASQ Quality Press at 800-248-1946, or write to ASQ Quality Press, P.O. Box 3005, Milwaukee, WI 53201-3005.

To place orders or to request a free copy of the ASQ Quality Press Publications Catalog, including ASQ membership information, call 800-248-1946. Visit our Web site at www.asq.org or http://qualitypress.asq.org.

∞ Printed on acid-free paper

Quality Press
600 N. Plankinton Avenue
Milwaukee, Wisconsin 53203
Call toll free 800-248-1946
Fax 414-272-1734
www.asq.org
http://qualitypress.asq.org
http://standardsgroup.asq.org
E-mail: authors@asq.org

Contents

Figures and Tables . . . . *vii*
Foreword . . . . *ix*
Preface . . . . *xiii*
Acknowledgments . . . . *xv*

Part I   The Corporate Death Spiral **1**

Chapter 1   The Corporate Death Spiral   1
What Is the Death Spiral?   2
The Warning Signs   6

Part II   The Warning Signs **11**

Chapter 2   Lost Purpose   11
What Is Purpose?   11
Profits and Stock Price   13
Holding the Organization Together   16
Identifying Lost Purpose   26
Summary   27
Chapter 3   Number Obsession   29
An Example of Doing It Right   29
It's a Matter of Importance   29
Stopping the Madness   34
Identifying Number Obsession   43
Summary   44
Chapter 4   Supplier Squeezing   45
Considering Total Cost   45
Supplier Turnover   49
What Is the Objective of Procurement?   55
Being a Great Customer   57
Most Understand, So What's the Problem?   58
Identifying Supplier Squeezing   58
Summary   60

vi   *Contents*

Chapter 5   Undervalued Employees   61
Cutting Assets to Improve Profit   62
Evaluating Performance   68
Respecting and Developing Employees   75
Continually Reduce Fear   78
Identifying Undervalued Employees   80
Summary   83
Chapter 6   Dirt, Clutter, and Damage   85
Damage and Breakdowns   85
Dirt and Clutter   90
Identifying Dirt, Clutter, and Damage   97
Summary   98
Chapter 7   Operational Fragmentation   99
Departmental Goals   99
What's Blocking Teamwork?   109
Defragmenting a Complex System   112
More Barriers to System Performance   114
It's a Matter of Leadership   117
How to Identify Operational Fragmentation   118
Summary   122

Part III   Addressing the Warning Signs **123**

Chapter 8   Improving the Organization's Health   123
The Need for Transformation   123
Requirements for Success   124

Appendix A   Internal Organizational Assessment **137**

Prioritizing Action   137
Warning Sign Prioritization   144

Appendix B   Statistical Process Control **145**

The Basic Statistical Formulas   146
Rules to Determine Stability of a System   147

Appendix C   The QFD Process **151**

Appendix D   Basic Reflection Questions **157**

Glossary *161*

Index *165*

Figures and Tables

Figure 1.1	Weakening of an organizational immune system.	3
Figure 1.2	The death spiral and crisis-mode management.	5
Table 1.1	Elements of a supportive improvement culture.	6
Table 1.2	Reasons for the lack of fundamental change in business.	9
Figure 2.1	Market capitalization values.	13
Table 2.1	Technology-induced product replacements.	24
Table 2.2	Customer needs in music media.	25
Table 3.1	Causes of immeasurable but significant losses.	30
Figure 3.1	Plant comparison chart.	34
Figure 3.2	Warranty expenses.	37
Figure 3.3	Warranty expenses with February result added.	37
Figure 3.4	On-time delivery performance.	38
Figure 3.5	Historical on-time delivery performance.	40
Figure 3.6	On-time delivery performance after improvement.	40
Table 4.1	Example of total cost analysis for a supplier.	46
Table 4.2	Total cost of purchased materials.	48
Table 4.3	Costs associated with purchase of supplies.	49
Table 4.4	Losses to a company resulting from delaying payments to a supplier.	53
Figure 5.1	Success and happy employees.	62
Table 5.1	The true cost of layoffs.	63
Table 5.2	Steps before workforce reductions.	65
Table 5.3	Intended benefits of performance appraisal systems.	73
Figure 5.2	Improving below-average employees.	75
Table 5.4	Benefits of developing managers from within.	76
Table 5.5	Typical fears within an organization.	78
Figure 6.1	Example of a preventive maintenance schedule.	89
Figure 6.2	Example of preventive maintenance instruction sheet (on back of maintenance schedule).	90

Table 6.1	Benefits of clean/organized work area.	92
Figure 6.3	Using outlines to identify locations.	93
Figure 6.4	Example of visual inventory control.	94
Figure 7.1	Overview of the PDSA process.	104
Figure 7.2	Lost-time accidents for North American plants.	107
Figure 7.3	Analysis of lost-time injury data.	107
Figure 7.4	Partial cause and effect analysis of joint injuries.	108
Table 7.1	Factors that affect worker performance.	119
Figure 8.1	Reflection and PDSA.	129
Figure 8.2	The affinity diagram.	134
Figure B.1	Charts depicting data from unstable systems.	148
Figure C.1	Level of involvement/leadership at each step of the process.	153
Figure C.2	QFD matrix example.	154
Figure C.3	Overview of the QFD process.	156

Foreword

Most people, if told that they are in a death spiral, would pay great attention to the doctor delivering that startling message, especially if told there was a way out. *Avoiding the Corporate Death Spiral: Recognizing and Eliminating the Signs of Decline* delivers the same message to leaders of the world's companies. It is to be hoped that corporate executives will take heed to the message of this book to avoid (or end) death spirals of their companies. But time is running out for many formerly great companies! We have all witnessed/are witnessing the decline of great companies that have been dying for many years. Various leaders are brought in to save the company, but the decline continues. Sometimes, a high-profile leader is brought in to save the company and a temporary lull in the decline occurs, only to be resumed when the miracle worker leaves. Intransigent workers, governmental action/inaction, and other forces are often blamed, but it is difficult for we who are leaders to look in the mirror and find the real source of problems. In a great many cases, the company in question could be saved and could prosper, but leaders do not pay heed to the rather simple (though not short-term) messages of this book.

Most companies have corporate mission statements, affirming in writing their reasons for being in business and their vision for the future. Instead of following their mission/vision and letting it drive their actions, however, many companies put the declarations on the wall and pay no heed in day-to-day operations. They never really decide who they are, who their customers are, and that their companies are in business to serve these customers. This type of mission/vision statement is a waste of time and paper. In my experience, shared vision is one of the most powerful tools at getting people to work together. Provided the course is right, this is vital to greatness.

Many companies that are in death spirals could know that they are there by the numbers that they generate, but these numbers either come too slowly or management will not acknowledge their problems. They suffer a long-term decline of market position, profitability, customer service levels, successful new products, and an increase in waste (inventory, scrap, rework, and so on). Invariably, if they take action, it is short term. But instead of getting to the root cause of problems that got them in trouble over a period of years, they try short-term actions to solve the problem. A common solution is to lay off workers, hire a fix-it CEO from the outside, and continue the practices that caused the problems. In many cases, there is an obsession with what the financial community thinks of the numbers, with no concern about what happens in the long term. Instead of taking action in areas where, many times, there seems to be no direct correlation to their problems (that is, promoting from within, training employees in areas critical to both present and future, creating an environment where all can work together for the betterment of the company and its stakeholders, and so on), there is a concern among the leadership of the company about improving the way the numbers look in the short term and not enough concern for long-term, permanent solutions. There are times, especially when a company is in deep trouble, that radical change is necessary. But there are no 90-day wonder solutions that will last.

On the other hand, numbers sometimes indicate that things are going poorly and such is not the case. In my own experience, a small company with which I was involved (and which had been growing rapidly) grew only 3 percent, (SG&A) expenses went up, and profits dropped. The underlying reason for this was the restructuring of the company that was needed to improve quality and customer service for the long term. In the succeeding 10-year period, the company grew at a compounded annual rate of over 15 percent, profit margins went up significantly, inventory turnover increased by a factor of five, and customer service level soared. Indeed, we were able to have our cake and eat it, but the company had to invest heavily in people and processes in order to realize its potential.

Another sure sign that companies are either in decline or stuck in a fair/poor position is their attitude toward suppliers. These companies usually treat all suppliers (or almost all) as short-term, disposable sources of parts supply at low initial price, and they always have an abundance of just-in-case suppliers. While initial price is important, in most cases (especially with key parts) working with good suppliers over the long term gains more for companies through time to market of new products, total cost of products through excellence of design, elimination of waste from excess inventory, efficiency of interfaces through mutual trust/effort, product quality, and the speed with which products are delivered to the end customer. Good supplier partners, like good user companies, have stable management and a desire to continually improve.

In the company referred to above, there was a temporary loss of growth and profitability due to investment in people and processes, but in the 10-year period addressed, sales grew by more than four times, while the number of suppliers shrank by two-thirds. Suppliers were key to satisfying customer's expectations for quality and service, and the cost of parts and supply infrastructure also decreased, belying conventional wisdom that there must be more than one supplier for key components. On the other hand, another company became so enchanted with price from suppliers that they dropped a long-term supplier who had such excellent quality and service that they delivered daily to the production line (without any inspection) in favor of a supplier who sold their parts at 10 percent less. The problem was that the new supplier had poor quality and delivery (and total costs were higher), and the company had to go back to the previous supplier (hat in hand) to beg them to supply their parts.

As stated above, declining companies are often characterized by executives who do not seem to have enough care for their most valuable resource: skilled, loyal employees. They treat employees somewhat like their suppliers: as a short-term, disposable source of labor. This results in poorer performance of the company than that which can be obtained through everyone working together for the betterment of the customers and other stakeholders. It always results in a distrust of management and waste. The leaders of the company should be there to serve the interests of the company, not to be put on a pedestal and served by other employees.

There has been much written about 5S, and this education is essential to great companies. Furthermore, one of the surest signs of the decline of a company can be seen by just walking through its operations. Not only will you see disinterested employees with their heads down, you will see clutter throughout. It means that no one (management nor the rest of the workforce) has pride in his/her work, and this will show in the products produced. On the other hand, when you walk through a great company, you invariably see clean, uncluttered work spaces and happy people.

Finally, and this may be the area of greatest importance, declining companies do not have people who work well together. Marketing people identify products needed (usually just features and specifications) and throw that over the fence to the engineers. One hopes that the marketing department has at least visited a few customers, although they should have intimate knowledge of various customer segments and their total needs. The engineers then design the product and throw it over the fence to manufacturing. Manufacturing then hopes that they can deal with suppliers that the engineers have chosen and that they can build the product (including training the workers) and get it to the market in the way and in the time desired by the customer (rare to non-existent in these companies). The job of the sales department is then to complain about poor delivery, lack of features, and poor product quality. This always creates waste, confusion, higher costs, and poorer service levels than if the barriers between departments were broken down and all worked together to deliver the goods and services that will delight the customer. Even after these companies have introduced products of poor quality or that don't meet their customer's needs, they still don't work together well to solve the problems created or realize why the problems exist. This attitude always results in stagnation/long-term decline.

Hopefully, the management of more and more companies will wake up to the lessons found in this book before time runs out for them, their fellow employees, their shareholders, and their customers.

Dennis G. Perkins
Group Vice President–Flow Products (Retired)
Emerson Electric Company

Preface

It's difficult to look at the world today and feel confident about the future. The newspapers seem to report daily about plant closures, layoffs, and bankruptcy filings somewhere in the world. Add to this a continually increasing U.S. trade deficit, soaring federal budget deficit, and the lowest levels of job satisfaction in history and the situation can seem downright scary.

Although these things are really nothing new to the world of business, they seem to be more prevalent today, possibly because some of the giants of industry, those companies that seemed to be virtually indestructible several years ago, are suffering. I spent the first 22 years of my life in Detroit, where the problems associated with competitiveness (or lack thereof) almost destroyed the city in the 1970s. Watching the decline in Detroit and the way it affected the people and families who relied on the automotive industry for their livelihoods had a profound affect on me and eventually led me to study why some companies suffer in response to one or more external events while others seem to escape with little or no damage.

My learning about organizations, leadership, and continual improvement has taken place over the last 30 years and resulted from a variety of things, including working with a number of organizations (both as an employee and a consultant); visiting and talking with the leaders of highly successful companies, as well as companies that have experienced decline in some form; and a good deal of training and education in leadership, psychology, strategy, and continual improvement.

My research led me to uncover several warning signs that identify practices which companies in a death spiral follow that companies with sustainable levels of success do not. I have further found that these practices are often in place years before a company enters a death spiral.

One of the interesting things about the warning signs is that they can show up in a company that is achieving financial success. What I found, though, is that the companies experiencing the warning signs tended to be negatively affected by external events to a much greater degree than those organizations that continually work to eliminate the warning signs. It is similar to the human body: someone with a weakened immune system can appear to be healthy as long as he or she is not exposed to some external condition that causes disease like bacteria, viruses, or environmental factors. Those who continually work to improve their overall health tend to strengthen their immune systems, however, and can withstand external events and conditions with less trouble.

PURPOSE OF THE BOOK

The purpose of this book is to present the warning signs of organizational decline and provide a method for leaders to identify and eliminate them before the organization enters a death spiral. The book will provide detailed explanations of each warning sign, including an explanation regarding how the sign contributes to the decline, and an assessment to determine the existence and extent of the signs within an organization.

The warning signs highlight symptoms of organizational decline. It is important for leaders to use the warning signs to assess the health of the organizations they lead and use the information to cure the systemic problems that interfere with long-term success. Improvement involves the application of a formal problem-solving process, including continual feedback to determine whether or not actions are resulting in the desired improvement.

Also included are suggestions for assessing an organization from the outside. Whether you are considering joining an organization as an employee or investing in its stock, it is important to understand the company's long-term prospects. As an example, shares in one Fortune 100 company that clearly exhibits the warning signs have been highly recommended by financial experts for investment over the last three years. If you followed the recommendation of the experts during this period, however, your investment would have lost 14 percent. On the other hand, if you had invested in shares of Toyota Motor Company (which is well known for producing quality products and continually developing its systems and people) over the same period, your investment would have grown by more than 92 percent. Unfortunately, most of the experts rated Toyota stock as a less attractive investment than the first company.

Another objective of this book is to help leaders create organizations that are fun places for people to work. The percentage of people today who are satisfied with their jobs, which is already at its lowest level in history, continues to fall. Most of us spend a large percentage of our waking hours at work (or worrying about work) and we have a right to enjoy our jobs. It is not fun to work in an organization in a death spiral. It is fun, however, to be a part of a company that is healthy and continually improves the value it provides to its customers. Continual efforts to identify and remove the warning signs presented in this book help make organizations healthy and great places to work.

Acknowledgments

Remembering everyone who has contributed to my knowledge and understanding of business and organizations would be an impossible task. I have learned something from virtually everyone with whom I interacted over the years, even those with whom I had disagreements.

There are people, however, who have had a significant impact on my life and in the writing of this book, for which I will be forever grateful.

First of all, I would like to thank my parents, Raymond and Catherine Stocker, for instilling in me a work ethic to constantly strive for perfection, even when it appears that others don't necessarily share in my beliefs.

The other people to whom I am grateful include:

W. Edwards Deming, for his wisdom, vision, and tireless efforts to teach people the responsibilities that go along with leading an organization, and for the development of the system of profound knowledge.

Gene Perkins of Emerson Electric Company, for taking his role as a leader seriously and accepting nothing less than complete commitment to continual improvement from those who worked in the organizations in which he led. Gene is always willing to help and teach those who are willing to learn, and I continue to call on him regularly for advice.

Dave Guerra, Dale Wood, and Jeff Lickson, for their friendship, insight, and countless hours of discussion on the topics of learning, organizations, and continual improvement. I would also like to thank them for the detailed feedback they provided on the many drafts of the manuscript for this book.

Jack Hillerich III, Bill Scherkenbach, Gary Convis, David Phillips, Jim Dale, James Schroth, Eddie Roberts, and Juri Jeske, for taking the time to review this book and provide valuable feedback which helped make the book more effective and much easier to read.

xvi   *Acknowledgments*

The great team at the American Society for Quality and Quality Press, for their willingness to take on the project, provide feedback on the manuscript, and give help and support along the way. Also, the people and organizations who gave me permission to reference their materials in the book including the American Production and Inventory Control Society, Scripps College, Bloomberg.com, M.D. Anderson Cancer Center, Motorola, Google, LTD Enterprises (yogiberra.com), and the W. Edwards Deming Institute.

Cathy Lewis and her team for their knowledge, connections, and work in getting the book in front of as many people as possible.

David Zerhusen, for help and support with the commercial and contractual aspects of publishing.

My wife, Tarra, for inspiration and believing in me even when I didn't believe in myself. I would also like to thank Tarra and my daughter, Emerald, for constantly reminding me what is important in life.

1

The Corporate Death Spiral

"Survival is optional."
—W. Edwards Deming[1]

There are no promises. Nowhere is it written that a company, regardless of how large it is or how successful it might seem to be, will survive. There have been too many highly visible and painful reminders of this fact over the last several years. The newspapers continue to report about large, well-known companies that at one time were extremely successful, falling apart seemingly overnight.

In reality, the decline of an organization is a process that usually takes several years and results from a number of actions, decisions, and behaviors that contribute to the demise. The highly complex nature of organizations and markets makes it difficult to determine what actions or events led to the problems being faced today. The decline can actually begin when times are good and continue for many years before it becomes obvious that the organization is in trouble. Unfortunately, when the decline becomes apparent, the leaders often shift into crisis mode and implement drastic actions to improve the situation that, although well intentioned, actually result in speeding up the rate of decline.

It is the beliefs and operating philosophy of the leaders of an organization which guide the strategies, decisions, and actions that ultimately determine the level of success that will be achieved today and into the future. Unfortunately, the philosophy governing many organizations today is leading them into a death spiral that will be difficult to escape. The high number of layoffs, bankruptcy filings, and budget cutbacks, along with the continually shrinking tenures of CEOs, all point to a bleak future. The reason that we are not in a full-fledged crisis and complete economic collapse is that so many companies are caught in the same spiral. If a company with serious

2   Chapter One

problems has competitors with serious problems, it is not very likely that people will notice or be overly concerned with improvement.

WHAT IS THE DEATH SPIRAL?

It is not difficult to identify the companies that are caught in a death spiral. Declining profits, shrinking market share, and mass layoffs are the most obvious signs. The list of companies that are spiraling downward include some of the perennial giants that, at one time, appeared highly successful and unstoppable.

When a company begins to decline, executives and analysts often blame the troubles on the economy, natural disasters, political situation, and a host of other external forces. Although these forces obviously have an effect on the success of a company, this does not explain why other organizations in the same industries and facing the same conditions continue to remain successful. Companies like Toyota, Southwest Airlines, Hillerich & Bradsby (makers of Louisville Slugger® baseball bats), and Nucor Steel are well known for their approaches to business and being enormously successful in industries where others, including some of those perennial giants, are fighting for survival.

These companies are governed by a philosophy that focuses on people—not spreadsheets, machines, or technology—to improve their ability to withstand external pressures. As an example of this focus, none of these companies have a history of laying off workers during troubled times.[2] By comparison, many competitors of these organizations resort to layoffs on a regular basis in response to shrinking sales revenues and profits. The focus on people is one of the reasons that these organizations have continued to grow during strong economic times and remain profitable during a weak economy, while many of their competitors continue to spiral downward into oblivion.

Entering the corporate death spiral is a two-stage process that begins with a weakening of the organization's immune system (Figure 1.1). This first stage is a repeating cycle that continually minimizes the contributions of people working in the organization.

Except in rare cases, a person joins a company highly motivated and ready to contribute to the company's success. It often doesn't take long in many organizations, however, for the person's motivation to begin to erode under the pressure of the policies, behaviors, and actions (or inactions) of management that result from a lack of trust in the ability and motives of workers.

The decreased motivation of the new worker (along with continued demotivation of the other workers) often becomes evident in the quality of

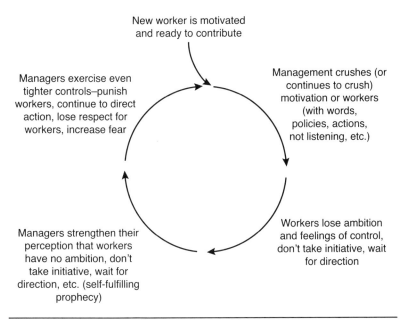

Figure 1.1 Weakening of an organizational immune system.

work performed or in the lack of initiative to take on new projects or go beyond the expectations of management. Recognizing this, management strengthens its perception that workers are not intrinsically motivated, are lazy, and are incapable of working without direction. Managers focus heavily on worker performance and can cite several examples supporting their belief that workers only respond to extrinsic motivators (positive and negative) like money, threats, and punishment, which in turn, strengthens the case for tighter controls.

What managers do not understand, however, is that they are directly responsible for creating this situation. Their philosophy regarding the need to closely manage and monitor workers has become a self-fulfilling prophecy. The people in the company now need tighter controls and clearer direction because of the barriers that management built that interfere with intrinsic motivation and the ability to take pride in work.

Weakening the Immune System

The control cycle continually repeats itself, gradually weakening the organization's immune system, which hampers its ability to withstand external pressures. If the market for the company's products or services is strong, the weakened immune system may not be immediately evident to the organization's management team. It is conceivable (and has been proven many times throughout history) that an immune-deficient company can remain profitable for a given period of time, thereby creating a false sense of security for managers and stockholders. Similar to the human body, an organization can appear to function well with a weakened immune system as long as it is not exposed to an external stimulus or event that can cause disease.

The problem occurs when one or more external events begin to negatively affect the company's revenues or earnings. These events could include a weakening economy, a new competitor or competitive technology, a change in political situation, or a host of other situations. Once one or more external events occurs, sales revenues or profits begin to slide, disease sets in, and managers begin to shift into crisis mode, thereby entering stage two of the spiral.

Although the steps in the cycle may differ slightly, the decline follows the same basic pattern in service companies as it does in manufacturing companies. It is actually more evident in services where a high percentage of workers are in direct contact with customers. There are examples of the death spiral today in automotive, airline, healthcare, retail, and a host of other industries.

Figure 1.2 presents the death spiral that results from a weakened immune system and crisis-mode management. When a drop in sales leads to declining profits, managers begin to take actions to reduce expenses to restore the company to an "acceptable" level of profitability. A usual first step in this process includes reducing or eliminating the expenses that don't lead to immediate and measurable results. Included in this first stage of cost cutting are often expenditures for training and development of people, and many longer-term product and/or service development projects.

If the immediate cost-cutting actions do not result in restoring profitability, the crisis-mode actions by management continue, which often include pressuring suppliers for reductions in price or lengthening of payment terms for purchased products and services. When this occurs, the quality of incoming materials and services tends to fall and lead times from suppliers increase. As a result, reduction in the cost of incoming materials and services shows up as a cost increase in other areas of the company and the net effect is either no change in profitability or, most likely, a further decline in profits.

Eventually, the situation for the company worsens until employee layoffs are implemented (although in many organizations, layoffs tend to be the first step to address weakening profitability). Layoffs are always followed by a drop in morale among remaining employees, which shows up in productivity and dealings with customers. This, along with the fact that the remaining employees are often not able to effectively keep up with cus-

Figure 1.2 The death spiral and crisis-mode management.

tomer demands, leads to decreased customer satisfaction and a further decline in sales revenues.

At this point, the death spiral is in full swing. Equipment and machine preventive maintenance is reduced (or eliminated) because of budget cutbacks, reduced resources, and a lack of interest by workers caused by reduced morale. As a result, machine and equipment breakdowns increase and the level of quality is reduced. Lower quality levels result in a continued decline in sales and profits, and the cycle starts all over again.

This death spiral continues until the culture is so sick that changing and improving the environment becomes a monumental task appearing to be insurmountable. If the spiral continues for several years, the problems can become so deeply-rooted that real improvement cannot occur without a fundamental change in the philosophy of the organization's leadership and a carefully planned strategy that shifts the organization from tight controls to an open, improvement-focused culture.

A *fundamental* change in philosophy refers to a shift in deeply held beliefs about people, business, and society. The shift can occur in response to a single event or series of events that causes a person to evaluate and reflect on his or her role in the world. For some people, the shift never takes place. Others may desire to make a change, but lack an understanding of

6 Chapter One

Table 1.1 Elements of a supportive improvement culture.

- Trust throughout the organization
- The ability to take pride in work performed
- Enthusiasm for improvement
- More focus on the operation or customers than on financial statements
- Continual development of people, leaders, and teams
- Purpose and values are clear, consistent, and believable

what it takes to make a change. The leader must feel strongly enough about the need to change to continually evaluate his or her own personal actions and behaviors. If it is a crisis that leads to a desire to change, the desire must be strong enough to continue on after the immediate crisis has passed. Without this level of change, the organization's systems and overall approach will not change and sustained improvement will not take place.

This is one of the biggest reasons for the failure of improvement initiatives like Six Sigma or lean manufacturing to achieve large-scale sustained improvement. These initiatives require a supportive culture that includes those elements listed in Table 1.1. Managers of companies in the midst of a death spiral do not understand the importance of these elements and tend to focus only on the technical aspects of improvement initiatives. As a result, attempts to improve fail because the culture is too weak to support the process.

Improving the cultural health of an organization is similar to improving the physical health of an individual. A person in declining health attempting an exercise program while continuing to smoke, eat the wrong foods, and maintain a stressful lifestyle will not significantly change his or her health. On the other hand, the person who understands the links between diet, exercise, and stress, and fundamentally changes his or her lifestyle to improve overall health (even though the benefits of the changes necessary cannot always be felt immediately), has a much better chance of success.

THE WARNING SIGNS

It is difficult for someone inside an organization to know that a company is in a death spiral. When you are close to the day-to-day operation, it is easy to get used to the problems and barriers to improvement and consider them to be normal. Many people have unfortunately become so accustomed to the ups and downs of a business, and the resulting layoffs and budget cuts that accompany the down cycles, that they don't see it as a problem. And to one who reads business periodicals regularly (and/or has been educated in a typical Western business school), layoffs and cutbacks can appear to be a normal part of business. Without a view of the entire company's operation, it is also difficult for someone to know whether an action taken in one part of the company is causing problems for another part. Perhaps a deeper problem is related to the fact that decline is independent of short-term performance and people are not accustomed to looking for problems when times are (or appear to be) good.

The obvious signs of declining organizational health include significant drops in sales, profits, and market share. Unfortunately, these signs don't usually appear until the death spiral has already begun and disease has set in, thereby making improvement much more difficult. The key to success is to avoid the death spiral by understanding the issues before the obvious signs appear.

There are several warning signs that identify an impending corporate death spiral. The warning signs bring to light the practices that weaken the organization's immune system and lead a company into decline before significant damage becomes obvious. The longer these signs are allowed to continue, the more deeply rooted the problems become and the more difficult it will be to pull out of the spiral.

Recognizing and Escaping the Death Spiral

There are several keys to successfully leading a company out of a death spiral. First, it is important to know the warning signs so you can attack the problems in the early stages before it kills the organization or seriously weakens its immune system. When one or more of the signs are evident, it is vital to fix the problems by understanding and attacking the *causes* of the warning signs instead of treating only the symptoms with short-term actions. Finally, by continually improving the culture and systems within the organization, you will build health and create a robust, disease-resistant company.

There are six warning signs of an organization in poor health. These signs can be considered leading indicators of disease that, left untreated, can result in deteriorating financial performance and other serious problems including layoffs, facility closings, and budget cuts. The warning signs of declining organizational health are as follows:

1. *Lost focus:* The people in the organization do not know why the company is in business and what they are attempting to accomplish, which results in focusing solely on personal definitions of success or financial measures (often leading to conflict between people and departments).

2. *Number obsession:* The leaders are heavily focused on financial indicators, and pay very little attention to the non-measurable aspects of the business (for example, morale,

8   *Chapter One*

culture, leadership development, and so on) that greatly affect the financial performance.

3. *Supplier squeezing:* Management considers the role of purchasing to be one of pressuring suppliers to reduce the price of incoming products and services, instead of developing long-term relationships with suppliers to continually improve quality, cost, and delivery.

4. *Undervalued employees:* The leaders do not place a high value on employees. Layoffs are common, fear is prevalent, and there is very little leadership development within the organization. Attempts are made to measure employee performance without taking into account non-measurable contributions.

5. *Dirt, clutter, and damage:* The workplace is dirty and unorganized, and buildings, property, and equipment are not well maintained.

6. *Operational fragmentation:* The level of teamwork is low and the company operates as a fragmented group of departments and people instead of as a single system working together to accomplish a common objective.

Leading a company out of a death spiral is a difficult task. The ability to reflect and openly discuss how actions and current systems may have led to the decline is absolutely necessary. Also required is an understanding that many commonly accepted business practices are contributing to the decline. This most likely requires moving out of a comfort zone and changing the systems and practices that are preventing the people in the company from achieving their full potential (as an example, throwing out traditional performance review systems and replacing them with something that helps people develop, grow, and contribute to the organization's success).

The Barriers to Improvement

The companies that have managed to escape or avoid the death spiral have been extremely successful from a financial perspective. The stories and success of organizations like Toyota, Southwest Airlines, Hillerich & Bradsby, and Gallery Furniture have been well publicized. Leaders at these companies have been more than willing to tell their stories in attempts to help others learn from their experiences. Unfortunately, the number of leaders who are willing or able to adopt a similar philosophy continues to remain relatively small.

There are several forces that prevent fundamental change from taking place in business today, even when the leader may actually want to change (see Table 1.2).

Table 1.2 Reasons for the lack of fundamental change in business.

(1)	**Lack of knowledge** The philosophy makes sense but you do not know where to begin or what to do.
(2)	**Fear** Change requires you to go against the traditional practices of leading an organization and requires you to leave your comfort zone. In effect, it requires you to break your programming and approach life and business in a much different way.
(3)	**Ego** Feelings that changing fundamental beliefs and practices includes the assumption that your previous philosophy or actions were wrong.
(4)	**Psychology void** The lack of working knowledge of psychology makes it difficult to implement a people-focused philosophy.

Lack of Knowledge. There are many executives who, although they agree in principle to a philosophy focused on people to strengthen the organization, don't know what to do to get started. Organizations are highly complex and attempts to initiate a transformation strategy have a greater chance of success when the leader has experience with the new philosophy. Without this type of experience and a clear understanding of what works, what doesn't, and why, it can be difficult to develop the plan to implement change.

Most leaders were not taught this philosophy in school to any depth, and, with a few exceptions, have no experience working with companies that practice a highly people-focused approach to business. This makes it difficult, but not impossible, to initiate the transformation. Those leaders who understand and practice the philosophy realize that transformation is a never-ending process and requires lifelong learning and continual practice to be successful.

Fear. Guiding an organization that continually focuses on strengthening its immune system runs counter to the traditional approach to leading an organization. When times get tough (for example, a drop in sales or earnings), it will be difficult to sell a no layoff policy to others. A Board of Directors or stockholders who do not understand the real costs of layoffs and other drastic cutbacks often think only of short-term performance, and will exert pressure to make quick or deep cuts in expenses. As a leader, if you are not fully committed to the philosophy or do not understand the philosophy well, you will have a difficult time defending your position. There may also be the tendency to go back to your comfort zone when times get tough and take actions that others expect you to take, even if you feel these actions did not really work well in the past to improve the immediate situation.

Ego. Some leaders may feel that implementing a new philosophy requires admitting that they were wrong in the past. Although life is a continual learning process, some leaders see it as a weakness to admit mistakes.

The philosophy itself consists of continually testing ideas and reflecting on results (that is, the Plan-Do-Study-Act (PDSA) cycle presented by W. Edwards Deming and Walter A. Shewhart). Once a leader understands this, he or she will begin to understand that true weakness results when he or she fails to learn from experience. It also may become clear to the transformed leader that he (as well as many around him) may have been promoted throughout the years for the wrong reasons. Understanding this is not a problem, but an opportunity to make things right in the future.

Psychology Void. Another factor that makes it difficult to implement a people-focused philosophy is the general lack of knowledge in psychology within the business world. A focus on people requires an understanding of people, including the motivations, needs, and passions that drive their actions.

If you start a company in which you are the only employee, this is obviously not an issue. The moment you add an employee, however, the organization becomes more complex and continues to become exponentially more complex with each new person added. As the number of barriers to teamwork grow, the ability to keep everyone together and focused on the purpose becomes more difficult.

By definition, a leader is someone who has followers. The ability to understand people is an absolute requirement for someone to be a leader, because without followers, there is no leader. It is also important to understand the difference between a boss and a leader in a business environment. Bosses are one of the factors that lead an organization into a death spiral, while leaders help pull it out.

NOTES

[1] Spoken by W. Edwards Deming during a four-day seminar July 14, 1992.

[2] Nucor and Southwest have never laid off workers and Toyota has not had a layoff since 1949 when, during the post-war reconstruction of Japan, the Bank of Japan forced a layoff in exchange for badly needed loans.

2

Lost Purpose

"If you don't know where you're going, you might not get there."
—Yogi Berra[1]

Definition

Forgetting why the company exists, resulting in people focusing on personal definitions of success (which often conflict with each other and are heavily financially driven).

The first and most obvious warning sign of organizational decline is the lack of a clear purpose that everyone understands and believes in. Purpose refers to mission (why the organization is in business) and vision (where the organization is headed). It's the basics of business management and, although it's been written about in books for more than 30 years, many leaders continue to downplay its importance.

The Cambridge Dictionary of American English[2] defines an *organization* as "a group whose members work together for a shared purpose in a continuing way." Following this definition, without a purpose there can be no organization; only a group of people focused on their own needs (which usually conflict with each other). This is the unfortunate situation in many organizations today and is one of the causes of people just putting in their hours and going home. Gaining the commitment of people requires giving them something clear and worthwhile with which to be committed.

WHAT IS PURPOSE?

What is the purpose of an organization? It's a philosophical question that usually invokes a variety of responses. When the question was asked in a survey of more than 300 working professionals, however, over two-thirds described the purpose of their organizations in financial terms (maximizing profit, earnings per share, stock price, and so on). In today's world where budget cutbacks and layoffs are common occurrences, it is understandable why people answer in this manner.

The leaders of many companies today are running their businesses as if money was the only factor. This is unfortunate because, if financial success is ever achieved in these companies, it will be short-lived, and will most likely come at the expense of employees and customers. When the focus is on financial performance, activities that don't provide immediate payback become much more expendable. Research, product or new service development, training, and leadership development are among the activities that become more difficult to justify when financial pressures mount.

Many leaders will justify short-term financial success by blaming the downturns on normal business cycles. Although cycles are a part of every business and industry, those companies that are driven to achieve their purpose seem to experience more and longer periods of success than those who aren't. On the other hand, companies that seem to lose their way often find that their growth periods get shorter and less frequent as the years go by. This pattern gives credence to the theory that long-term success is the direct result of effective leadership, while intermittent success is due to economic conditions.

Figure 2.1 uses market capitalization to demonstrate the results of two companies known for staying focused on a clear purpose related to something other than financial measures. The graphs show the market value of shares of Toyota Motor Company (Figure 2.1a) and Southwest Airlines (Figure 2.1b) as compared to others within their respective industries. Although there are a variety of measures to assess the success of an organization, market capitalization was chosen because it demonstrates how the investment community values a company. These two organizations actually lead their industries in virtually every financial measure.

As shown in Figure 2.1, the investment community values these two companies significantly more than that of their competitors. At the time of this analysis, the market capitalization value of Southwest Airlines was three times the combined values of the other major U.S. airlines, and Toyota's value was significantly higher than the other auto manufacturers (and about one-third higher than the combined values of the *Big 3* automakers). These examples demonstrate the value that the investment community places on companies with sustained levels of success—a direct result of effective leadership. The results also show that investors, who are often identified as the cause for the short-term focus of many companies, highly value a long-term approach to business.

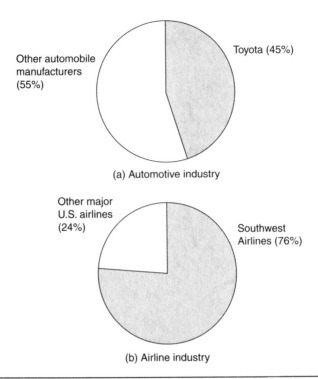

Figure 2.1 Market capitalization values.

There are only a few organizations that dominate an industry's market capital the way Toyota and Southwest Airlines do. The intermittent periods of success experienced by most organizations most likely lead many investors to pressure leaders to take actions that will boost stock prices in the present, with little or no regard to the effects on the future of the company.

PROFITS AND STOCK PRICE

Those who preach that profit (or any other financial measure) is not the purpose of organizations are often unfairly characterized as living in a fantasy world where profits do not matter. Profits are extremely important to a business. Without profits, the business will die, but profit is *not* the reason for the organization's existence.

James Collins and Jerry Porras, in their book, *Built to Last: Successful Habits of Visionary Companies*[3], compare profits to a company with oxygen,

14 *Chapter Two*

food, water, and blood to a human being. Although we need these things to survive, they are *not* the purpose of our existence or the main focus of our lives.

People who feel that profit is the reason businesses exist need to define the scope of profit. Is it profit for today? This month? This year? Or is it profit for the next 5–10 years? It makes a difference because the period in question affects the decisions made today. Organizations that continually hire and layoff workers in response to business cycles are obviously focusing on this year's profits with little or no regard to future profits. Only a clear purpose, defined in terms of a service that people value, can enable the company to achieve long-term financial success.

It's a philosophical but important difference: leaders who focus on profit manage differently than those who focus on serving customers. An executive who wants profits to increase now can do so by eliminating training programs, cutting product or service development, and reducing technical support, because these are costs that don't necessarily generate any revenue or profits right now. Managers who cut the activities that don't produce financial results in the short term obviously don't worry about the future. Many figure they will deal with the future when it becomes the present. It is even more likely that they will move elsewhere before the future gets here anyway, only to leave the problems they created to the next manager to deal with. A focus on profit as the purpose also tends to create tension between stockholders and employees instead of bringing them together as a team. Short-term thinking becomes dominant in decision making and employees, especially those whose efforts do not appear to directly contribute to the profitability in the short term, become expendable. When this occurs, the employees, customers, and stockholders all lose. Executives who focus on serving customers understand the value of training, development, and the other aforementioned activities that strengthen the organization and see them as investments that will result in improved quality, customer satisfaction, and continued profits for the long term.

Are We a Part of the Problem?

In many ways, Western culture has led managers to believe that making money is the purpose of organizations. Stock ownership, which used to be considered a long-term investment, has become very short term (daily or even hourly in some circumstances). Investors in general place heavy emphasis on quarterly earnings reports. Stock prices depend largely on the results of the previous quarter, and projections for the coming quarter and rest of the year. Earnings projections for the next quarter seem to have more of an effect on stock price than plans and projections for the next 1–5 years. We put our stocks on our computer screens so we can watch their prices throughout the day. We feel good when prices go up and sometimes wonder why we didn't sell the previous day when prices fall. Many companies even display their stock prices on electronic boards or monitors within their facilities to show up-to-the-minute prices, obviously hoping to keep their employees focused on the stock price as they make decisions and take actions throughout the day.

Laying off workers, which is one of the most culturally devastating actions a company can take, usually results in a short-term increase in the company's stock price. When this happens, we as investors are effectively rewarding the company for poor leadership.

Our collective tendency to buy and sell stocks on a frequent basis puts enormous pressure on company executives to mortgage the future in order to make today look better. And in today's world, many CEOs feel that if they don't worry about today, they probably won't need to concern themselves with the future.

Investor pressures also make boards of directors worry more about the latest results than the internal operations and future of the company. Bonus plans that are closely tied to stock price, or some other financial indicator that affects stock price, are commonplace in organizations and only serve to compound the problem of executive emphasis on short-term financial measures, instead of improving the products or services, people, and systems within the organization. It is not uncommon to read articles about bonus plans that have made executives rich and left organizations in shambles.

Newspapers have recently been full of examples of very large companies that have abandoned their purpose to become money machines, (produce money without offering any tangible product or service). The heavy focus of these companies on financial aspects has led to very creative and sometimes illegal ways of achieving what they defined as success. Even when no laws are broken, money machines tend to have very short lives, and over the long term are much more damaging than beneficial to society. Although longer-term investors clearly value organizations with a longer-term focus (as shown in Figure 2.1), there is a large percentage of investors who want quick returns without concern for the potential damage it can cause for the organizations in which they invest or the economy as a whole.

The Investment Process: A Simple Example

A person starts a business because he perceives a need that relates to something he does well. If the business is successful, he will need capital in order to expand and take care of the growing list of customers.

After seeing the success and potential for growth in the business, you decide to give him the money he needs. Instead of a loan, however, you give him the money in exchange for a percentage of the business.

16 *Chapter Two*

You invest in his business because you believe in what he does and you expect the success he has achieved to continue into the future, leading to financial success for you.

If the founder abandons the purpose that he has had since the beginning, and turns his focus to profits and keeping *you* happy instead of his customers, what do you think the chances are that the company, and you, will reap financial benefit?

Although this example is overly simplified, it describes what happens in the world today. Investors should buy stock because they believe in the company and that the way management is running the business will lead to continued success. Profits, although a measure of how well the organization is achieving its purpose, have nothing to do with the organization's purpose. Pressuring management to take actions that result in abandoning the company's purpose is irresponsible and has negative long-term consequences for everyone (including employees, stockholders, customers, suppliers, and society). On the other hand, stockholders should fight to protect their investment if they see the company's leaders abandoning the purpose in favor of short-term returns.

HOLDING THE ORGANIZATION TOGETHER

A clear and unchanging purpose becomes the glue that holds the organization together. It's difficult for most people to be objective enough to think outside of their area of specialization. Accounting professionals generally see the organization from a financial perspective; salespeople view the organization from a sales perspective; and so on. Unless the purpose of the organization is clear, people will tend to think of their own areas as the purpose, instead of as a component of a larger system with a greater purpose. Battles will ensue between areas as each tries to achieve its own purpose.

W. Edwards Deming, the management and statistical consultant who introduced the concept of continual improvement and transformation to many Japanese companies in the 1950s, wrote, "Left to themselves . . . components become selfish, competitive, independent profit centres, and thus destroy the system."[4] To have a system, there must be a purpose, which was the reason for the system's creation. If there is no purpose, or if the organization has forgotten its purpose, the individuals will make assumptions about the purpose. Because the assumed purpose will be different for each person depending on their own perspective, competition within the company will occur, resulting in the organization's decline.

Manufacturing people who are focused on dollars shipped instead of customer commitments or quality is an example of Deming's reference to *independent profit centers*. Other examples include salespeople making commitments that the company cannot meet in order to meet forecasts; and purchasing agents buying the lowest cost materials or supplies without regard to the effect they have on the operation or the customer. People in these areas begin to think of their objective as generating profit (by maximizing output, reducing costs, and so on) without regard to the company as a whole.

There are unfortunately many more examples like these in business today that result in increased costs and decreased quality for the company, and lowered job satisfaction for the employees. The people working in the companies in these examples are not bad workers. They are specialists in need of a common purpose to pull their talents together and get them moving in the same direction. People naturally look for ways to motivate themselves, and if there isn't a clear overall purpose for the organization, they will create one based on their own perspective.

A Worthwhile Purpose

Regardless of position or level in the organization, people spend a significant percentage of their lives at work. And those who are in touch with their own passions and purpose like to feel that they are making a positive contribution to society in exchange for the large amount of time they invest.

When the organization has no apparent purpose, however, and people don't feel like they are making a worthwhile contribution, they may begin to look outside of work for ways to satisfy their needs. This will result in using their jobs as a means to pay the bills, and fund outside, more rewarding activities. When this happens, money (in terms of wages, salaries, or bonuses) becomes the focus and the measure of success, instead of a company-wide measure.

There have been numerous studies conducted and written about over the years comparing intrinsic and extrinsic motivation[5,6]. Most of these studies have concluded that intrinsic motivation is much more powerful than extrinsic motivation. Another common conclusion of these studies is that the more a person is motivated with extrinsic methods, the more he or she becomes disconnected with intrinsic needs. Studies have also concluded that extrinsic motivators need to be continually increased to achieve the same level of response.

Following this logic, the longer the organization has gone without a connection to its purpose, the more difficult it will be to reconnect and align people with the purpose. Some people will be skeptical and see the effort as another fad that will go away as the business environment changes or a crisis occurs. In many cases, this skeptical attitude toward the purpose is a defense mechanism that has been developed through repeated management inconsistency. Many people find it easier to take a *wait and see* approach to a new

18 *Chapter Two*

direction, instead of making an emotional investment that may lead to disappointment when the idea is abandoned in the future. Only after the leaders demonstrate consistency in their commitment to the purpose (through good times *and* bad) will these people begin to believe.

There will be another group of people who may want to follow the purpose, but will have difficulty breaking old habits. These people don't think about their own behavior enough to understand when their actions are counter to the purpose of the organization. This group needs a good deal of feedback, in addition to learning how to reflect on their own behaviors, to effectively contribute to the organization. They will need to be taught how to listen to others, and step outside of themselves long enough to comprehend when their words and actions prevent the purpose from taking hold.

There will also be a small group of people who are not able to commit to the organization's purpose. There may be a variety of reasons for this, including no personal interest in the organization's purpose; lack of clarity of the person's own purpose and direction (that is, not understanding one's own intrinsic motivators); anger from not being involved in the process of developing the purpose; or a variety of other reasons that are very complex and will be difficult to resolve. This group of people will most likely leave the organization if they perceive that management is serious about the chosen direction.

The key to aligning the people with the organization's purpose is consistent commitment by the leaders. This may sound cliché, but it's vital and, unfortunately, often misunderstood. The leaders must be passionate about the purpose. They must realize that their personal success is closely tied to the organization's success in aligning with and achieving the purpose.

To be successful, the leader needs to clearly understand his or her personal passions, and be able to align those passions with the organization's purpose. This is much easier when the leader is the founder of the organization than when the leader is several years or generations removed from the founder. Even founders have trouble, however, moving the organization forward when it appears to the founder that the organization has achieved its original purpose.

Giving Meaning and Constancy to the Organization

To be effective, an organization's purpose needs to clearly identify the positive contribution that the company makes to society (that is, be value focused) and remain constant into the future. Without these criteria, people will not be inspired and, therefore, not commited to achieving it.

Some purpose statements that meet the criteria of being clear, inspiring, and value focused include the following:

> *"I will build a motor car for the great multitude. It will be large enough for the family, but small enough for the individual to run*

and care for. It will be constructed of the best materials, by the best men to be hired, after the simplest designs that modern engineering can devise. But it will be so low in price that no man making a good salary will be unable to own one—and to enjoy with his family the blessing of hours of pleasure in God's great open spaces."

Henry Ford (1907)[7]

"The Boeing policy is to so develop airplane design and construction that today's spectacular feat of bravery will become tomorrow's accepted mode of speedy transportation—inexpensive, dependable, safe!"

Boeing (written in 1927)[8]

"Google's mission is to organize the world's information and make it universally accessible and useful."

Google[9]

"The mission of the University of Texas M. D. Anderson Cancer Center is to eliminate cancer in Texas, the nation, and the world through outstanding programs that integrate patient care, research, and prevention, and through education for undergraduate and graduate students, trainees, professionals, employees, and the public."

M. D. Anderson Cancer Center[10]

"The mission of Scripps College is to educate women to develop their intellect and talents through active participation in a community of scholars, so that as graduates they may contribute to society through public and private lives of leadership, service, integrity, and creativity."

Scripps College[11]

The preceding statements of purpose were the basis of some very successful organizations. Each of these organizations has experienced tremendous success over the years, although none of them specifically makes reference to financial returns in its reason for existence. For some reason, however, many executives today feel they must include a reference to returns to shareholders within their statements. It is critical to understand that financial returns *are* important for survival, but they are *not* the reason for a company's existence. People will not be inspired to work hard to make money for someone else. They will, however, be inspired by working on something that is a challenge and/or they see as beneficial to society. Making reference to the shareholders in a mission statement while ignoring the other stakeholders communicates to the people within the organization that shareholders are

20 *Chapter Two*

more important than the other components of the system. When this occurs, competition is created between shareholders and employees. It is a competition where both parties lose.

Henry Ford's drive to build a car that the masses could afford was inspiring at the time. Even though many thought it was not possible, those who did took a personal stake in making the vision a reality. The problems Ford experienced after the Model T may have been due to the fact that he had the company so focused, and he was so successful in achieving his original vision, that he lost direction, which is a common problem faced by entrepreneurs.

Boeing's vision was considered even more outrageous than Henry Ford's, but it was just as inspiring to those who believed it could happen and wanted to be a part of it. According to the Boeing company website (www.boeing.com), *Scientific American* magazine wrote in 1910, "to affirm that the airplane is going to revolutionize the future is to be guilty of the wildest exaggeration." It is this type of belief that fueled the inspiration of those who worked with William Boeing in the beginning.

The story of Google's success has been written about for many years. By continually developing its technology in pursuit of its purpose, it has been able to grow and become extremely successful at a time when competitors suffered. Today, the company continues to grow as it looks for better ways to organize and communicate information.

The clarity of the mission statement for M. D. Anderson Cancer Center in Houston, Texas, has helped direct their efforts not only to treating cancer, but eliminating it. This is very important for the direction of a health care facility, as most are focused on treating disease rather than eliminating or preventing illness. The focus on curing cancer is the foundation for much of M. D. Anderson's success and its reputation as one of the top cancer centers in the world.

Like the previous examples, it was an inspirational vision that brought people together to build Scripps College in Claremont, California, into a successful educational institution. In the early 1900s, Ellen Browning Scripps dreamed of a college setting that would be ideally suited to educate women. Her vision and the efforts of many who believed in the vision led to the development of the college that is one of the most highly respected liberal arts institutions in the United States.

Reinventing the purpose refers to adjusting the vision to account for the changes in the external environment and the degree to which the organization has achieved its current vision. This is not something that needs to occur on a monthly or even yearly basis, but it should be reviewed regularly to determine its continued relevance to the company and the markets it serves.

The organization's mission, however, should not change. Although reviewing it regularly is useful for a variety of reasons, it is the foundation of the company and changing it that could result in major problems for the organization. There may be times when an organization loses its purpose for so long that it has no connection with (or competencies for) its original mission. In these cases, departure from the original mission may be justified to get the company headed in some type of consistent direction. Continental Airlines went through this type of rebirth during the 1990s under the leadership of Gordon Bethune. Throughout its history (which included mergers and bankruptcy protection) Continental appeared to have lost its way. Bethune was able to unite the organization behind a single purpose, using Fly to Win, Fund the Future, Make Reliability a Reality, and Working Together as the four cornerstones of their plan to move forward.

Having a clear purpose does several things for an organization. First of all, it attracts people to the organization who have similar interests and passions. During the recruiting process, it gives the company another dimension with which to screen job candidates. It also gives the candidate a very important basis with which to screen the company.

Another important benefit of a clear purpose is that it gives a basis for reviewing activities in the organization to determine whether or not they add value. This is a critical exercise, but one that many leaders choose to ignore. If the company has a product line or participates in a business that doesn't support its purpose, it needs to make a change. If it doesn't change, these activities will drain resources from vital activities and interfere with the core business. Even when managers see this happening, however, there is often reluctance to take action, which is unfortunately a sign of wavering commitment to the purpose.

When management reviews a business segment (or product line) to determine its continuing viability, it needs to understand how the segment supports the company's purpose. Unfortunately, the decision is usually based on purely financial measures (profit, earnings, and so on), which often leads to losing touch with the organization's purpose, causing future problems for the company.

Mergers Add to the Complexity

Mergers and acquisitions add a great deal of complexity to the challenge of keeping an organization's purpose alive. Although it's not always a good thing for employees, customers, or stockholders, mergers have become a normal part of the business world today. When one organization acquires another, one of three scenarios can occur: status quo; subsidiary dilution; or parent poisoning.

In the first scenario, the acquired company is left alone by the parent to continue to operate as it had prior to the acquisition. Although this situation rarely occurs, in many ways it probably makes the most sense of the scenarios.

If the parent makes an acquisition because of the success the company has had, or to have access to specific technical knowledge, it only makes sense to leave the company's purpose unchanged. Interfering with or changing the purpose or systems usually results in driving key people out of the company and altering the company's culture, which can have long-lasting and devastating consequences. There is nothing wrong with making logical adjustments to operations to take advantage of the larger system in which the subsidiary now operates, but even this should be done with extreme care. Not accounting for the company's purpose and culture is one of the quickest ways to kill the subsidiary and prevent the merger from producing long-term benefit for all involved.

Perhaps the most common and unfortunate scenario with acquisitions is dilution of the subsidiary's purpose. The parent company either forces its purpose onto the acquired company, or the subsidiary's purpose is de-emphasized to the point of becoming meaningless.

Although it may make sense to fold the new company into the purpose of the parent when the acquired company produces the same products and serves the same markets, it must be done very carefully. The change effort must take into account the culture of the acquired company and the people must not feel disrespected in the process. It's a slow process that must be carefully planned and implemented.

Dilution of purpose in the acquired company has become a common practice in recent years. During the 1990s and early 2000s, companies were acquired for a variety of reasons including large cash reserves, feeding the egos of executives, or simply to show investors large growth rates. Whether acquiring a company made sense from a technological, market, or cultural perspective had less to do with the decision than the effect to the parent company's financial statements. There are numerous examples of organizations being acquired, only to be dismantled little by little by the parent company. Spending considered *nonessential* by the parent company is eliminated or greatly reduced (including product development, training, and quality improvement activities), so the subsidiary could contribute more cash to the parent in the short term. In these instances, financial gains to investors (and executives of the parent company) are short-lived, and result in losses for the employees and customers of the acquired company.

Too often, the acquiring company will attempt to make itself look good by achieving quick results from the merger. This leads to some very short-term decisions that generate an illusion of success, but end up forfeiting the subsidiary's future. By the time the problems show up in the company's performance, so much time has passed and so much has happened that it is difficult to link the past actions with current results.

Perhaps the least common but most damaging scenario for mergers is *parent poisoning*, which occurs when the acquired company poisons the parent by making it forget its own mission, vision, and values. In a recent example, a company well known in its industry for high quality products and innovation purchased one of its competitors. The competitor had a significant market share in one of the company's businesses but was known throughout the industry as a highly political organization with a predatory and destructive culture. For several years, this competitor had exhibited signs of an organization that had forgotten its reason for existence. Its employees, customers, and suppliers were increasingly becoming dissatisfied with the company.

The cultural weaknesses were so strong in the acquired company that, not long after the acquisition, the parent began exhibiting similar characteristics. This most likely occurred because the leaders were overwhelmed with the magnitude of the problems at the subsidiary organization and lost focus on the parent company. The result was lower performance by the new, combined company and the loss of several key management and technical people who became disenchanted with the new organization.

Organizations where leaders understand the complexity of culture, and its effect on company performance, tend to grow managers from within rather than through acquisition. Toyota[12] is probably the best known company that has grown without acquisition. The strategy at Toyota is to expand carefully their operations from within to respond to sales growth and market expansion. Although expanding a culture is a very sensitive and difficult process, it is much easier than dealing with the problems and difficulties that arise from attempting to merge another culture into an existing organization.

The Product Is Not the Purpose

The warning sign of lost focus also exists when a manufacturing or distribution organization defines its purpose in terms of the product it sells instead of the need the product serves. Although a very important but often overlooked point, the product is how the company serves its customers, which enables it to meet its purpose, but it is not its purpose. In other words, the purpose is the *what* and the product is the *how*.

Technology changes much too quickly to expect any product to last indefinitely. The list of products that have been replaced by technology is long and continues to grow each day. As shown in Table 2.1, a product does not even need to be less expensive to replace another, as long as it meets the intended need better. The company that defines itself by a product loses its identity when innovations occur and technology changes.

It is interesting to note that, in many cases, the customer may even be completely satisfied with the product being offered. Their needs are met, as far as they know, and there is no reason to believe that they will switch to another product. When the new technology is introduced that meets their true need better, however, they will not hesitate to jump to the new product.

24 *Chapter Two*

Table 2.1 Technology-induced product replacements.

Product	Replaced by
Typewriter	Word processing software
Slide rule	Calculator
Carburetor	Fuel injector
Ice cube tray	Electric icemaker
Gas lamps	Electric lights
Phonograph record	Compact disc
Compact disc player	MP3 player
Personal organizers	PDAs
VHS video tape	DVD
Portable CD player/radio	MP3 player
Sand filtration (swimming pools)	Cartridge filter

The reason for this is that the customer doesn't always understand their own real need with the products they purchase. When asked, they will define their needs in terms of what producers have given them in the past. They don't know what is possible, so they won't necessarily be able to ask for innovations or breakthrough features in the products they purchase.

Compact discs (CD) and CD players are an excellent example of this phenomenon. Customers learned to live with the inherent problems of vinyl recordings and were generally satisfied. There were probably very few, if any, customers who would have asked for portable players to be able to listen while walking or the ability to program the player to automatically skip, repeat, and/or reorder the songs. Once CDs and CD players were introduced, however, the death of vinyl records and phonographs was swift (see Table 2.2). To further the example, CDs appear to be experiencing a serious challenge from MP3 players.

The Need for Passion

So what makes the purpose clear? Thousands of organizations have developed and communicated purpose statements, sometimes at considerable expense. Why, then, are some extremely successful at sticking to their purpose, while most are not? Why are most efforts to establish the purpose doomed to fail from the beginning?

Table 2.2 Customer needs in music media.

General Need			
Hear music with a high quality sound, when I want, with as little effort as possible.			
Records and cassette tapes appeared to meet the needs of customers until the compact disc was introduced. Compact discs were more expensive than cassette tapes and vinyl records, and required customers to purchase new audio equipment, but led to obsolescence of both because it met the needs of customers much better (see below).			
Need	**CD**	**Vinyl**	**Cassette**
Portability	+	−	−
Programmability	+	−	−
Durability	+	−	−
Ease of changing albums	+	−	+
Easy to store	+	−	+
More music	+	−	−

One answer lies in the passion the leaders have for the organization's purpose. If the leaders are not passionate about the purpose, no matter how much they try, they will be unable to commit to it, and they will continually make decisions and take actions that are not aligned with the stated direction of the company.

Acting committed to a purpose during good times is easy, even when you're not passionate about it. True commitment during bad times, however, is only possible when your personal passions are closely linked with the purpose of the organization. When you're passionate about a cause, the economic conditions are irrelevant. Although conditions will obviously influence some of the decisions you make, you will not respond to the conditions by abandoning the purpose of the company.

All of this assumes that the purpose of the organization addresses a need in the marketplace. If the company's purpose is to serve a need that doesn't exist or is not prevalent enough to economically support the company, it will not be successful. Sometimes, however, following a course requires the creativity to create opportunities for market expansion or product and service innovations that enable the company to be successful, even when the opportunities are not immediately apparent.

The passion and purpose at Southwest Airlines led them to expand their market by bringing air travel to people who previously didn't have access to

26 Chapter Two

it before because of financial or geographical constraints. Honda and Toyota expanded the market for luxury cars by offering models that had features that were comparable to (or better than) existing models of high-end automobile manufacturers, but at lower prices.

IDENTIFYING LOST PURPOSE

If you're working in an organization, it is fairly easy to identify whether or not the purpose is clear. Conflicting messages or actions that run counter to the stated purpose are clear indications that the organization doesn't understand its reason for existence. Actions of management that demonstrate the sole purpose of the organization as making money also indicate the lack of understanding of the company's reason for existence and is a sign of organizational decline.

What to do if you identify this warning sign depends on your individual circumstances. If you feel you're in a position to change the company's culture, it is your responsibility to re-establish the purpose of the organization and work to refocus the people toward its achievement. Even if you have to start small (that is, within a team or department), this is potentially the most rewarding alternative. Giving meaning to the jobs people have and watching the team pull together for a common purpose is one of the most rewarding (and important) responsibilities of a leader.

The other obvious choices for you, if you find your company has no clear or meaningful purpose, include leaving the organization or staying and hoping things will change.

If you're pursuing a job with a company, it's important to ask about the company's purpose during the interviewing process. Most people tend to forget that they need to interview the company at the same time the company is interviewing them.

During the interviews, be wary of the company if you receive any of the following:

- Conflicting or different answers from different people

- Confusion about what you're asking

- Answers focused on money

If you've made the decision to leave your present job to pursue another, you are doing yourself a disservice if you don't make sure you are going into a better organization. Too often, people are so desperate to get a job that they ignore the signs of organizational decline, which are sometimes clearly evident and move from one death spiral to another.

Perhaps the person who will have the most difficulty identifying this warning sign is a potential investor. Without being inside of the company, it's very difficult to understand the culture and know whether or not the company has a clear purpose.

The first step is to *read* the annual report. Too often, people tend to skip the text in a report, and jump to the numbers to begin calculating ratios and looking at growth rates (others never even open the annual reports from companies in which they invest money). If there's anything to be learned from the events in recent years, it's that the numbers don't tell the whole picture.

Look for clues in the body of the report about how well the leaders understand their purpose. Read the messages from the Chairman and CEO. Do they talk about the company's purpose or are they focused on financial measures (cost cutting, growth rates, and so on)?

Attempt to understand the makeup of the management team and the board of directors to see if they are heavily weighted toward financial expertise versus technical knowledge. Often, companies will list the names and credentials of their management team on their website. The qualifications and experience of those who serve on the Board of Directors of a company are listed in the proxy material during elections.

If the company serves consumer markets, use your own experience as a gauge of how well they understand their purpose. It really doesn't make sense to invest in a company when you don't believe in the company's products. Financial success for a company that provides poor quality products and services is a very short-term event.

Other sources of information include product and service quality studies. A rating that is consistently near the top for the products and services of a company is usually a good indication that management understands the company's purpose and is serious about serving its customers.

This approach to investing takes more time than conventional ways to analyze a company, but it greatly improves the ability to see a warning sign before investing money.

SUMMARY

Of all the warning signs of impending trouble, lack of clear purpose is probably the most significant because it relates in some way to the other signs of trouble. A company that does not know why it exists will probably not have to ponder the question for long. There are plenty of other organizations that are ready and willing to serve its customers, take away its business, and drive the company to extinction. One important step in pulling an organization out of a death spiral is to refocus around the purpose. A clear and meaningful purpose will draw people together and provide a foundation for the survival of the company. It will also help clarify which activities are necessary and which are truly non-essential.

It is important to note that, although focus on the purpose is an absolute requirement for long-term success, it does not guarantee success. The leaders of the company need to know how to strengthen the organization to enable it to achieve its purpose. Understanding the existence and extent of the other warning signs is necessary, along with the ability to determine the causes for their existence and the ability to undertake actions to eliminate them.

NOTES

[1] Credited to Yogi Berra, but has not been published per LTD Enterprises (www.yogiberra.com).

[2] *Cambridge Dictionary of American English.* 1999. Cambridge, UK: Cambridge University Press.

[3] Collins, James, and Jerry Porras. 1994. *Built to Last: Successful Habits of Visionary Companies.* New York: Harper Business Essentials (HarperCollins).

[4] Deming, W. Edwards. 1994. *The New Economics for Industry, Government, Education.* Cambridge, MA, MIT Press, p. 50.

[5] Kohn, Alfie. 1998. "Challenging Behaviorist Dogma: Myths About Money and Motivation." *Compensation & Benefits Review,* March/April.

[6] Herzberg, Frederick. 2003. "One More Time: How Do You Motivate Employees." *Harvard Business Review,* January 1.

[7] Lacey, Robert. 1986. *Ford: The Men and the Machine.* Boston: Little, Brown, p. 87.

[8] Associates in Process Improvement. 1999. *Quality as a Business Strategy*, Austin, TX: Author.

[9] From the Google website (www.google.com).

[10] From the M. D. Anderson website (www.mdanderson.org).

[11] From the Scripps College website (www.scrippscol.edu).

[12] Bodek, Norman. 2003. "Quality Conversation with Gary Convis: The Toyota Executive Explains the Human Side of Manufacturing." *Quality Digest,* November.

3

Number Obsession

*Not everything that counts can be counted, and not
everything that can be counted, counts.*
—Albert Einstein

Definition

*Focusing heavily on financial indicators while paying little or no
attention to the non-measurable aspects of a business (for example, morale, culture, leadership development, and so on).*

AN EXAMPLE OF DOING IT RIGHT

Herb Kelleher, Chairman and ex-CEO of Southwest Airlines, credits the people at the company, rather than his financial expertise, for the success of the airline. Although financial matters are obviously important when making major decisions, they do not dominate the thought process.

In a Leader to Leader Institute article[1], Kelleher described the planning process used at Southwest. ". . . rather than trying to predict what we'll do, we try to define who we are and what we want in terms of market niche, operational strategy, and financial health. We reflect, observe, debate—and we don't use our calculators."

IT'S A MATTER OF IMPORTANCE

The quickest way to gain an understanding of what's important to a company is to identify the measures that the leaders pay attention to the most. If most (or all) of the indicators are financial in nature and they dominate the

30 *Chapter Three*

discussion during meetings, it is a sign that the leaders are focused on numbers instead of people and systems. Basically, if the leaders spend more time with spreadsheets than people, they are number-obsessed. The development of the spreadsheet may actually have been one of the worst things that has ever happened to business. What should have become a great tool for companies has turned into an obsession of managers and put up a wall between management and the people in many organizations.

The problem with this approach is, as W. Edwards Deming stated repeatedly, the most significant costs to the organization (referred to by Deming as *the heavy losses*) cannot be measured. Table 3.1 presents a list of some of the major costs to an organization that cannot be measured, but if not managed and continually reduced can lead an organization into a death spiral.

Although some of the issues listed in Table 3.1 can be measured (for example, employee satisfaction or employee turnover), the costs associated with problems with these issues are impossible to ascertain. For example, the cost to the company resulting from a lack of teamwork is impossible to measure, although most would agree that it is very large.

Robert Kaplan and David Norton introduced the concept of a balanced scorecard for businesses in a Harvard Business Review article in 1996.[2] Under the balanced scorecard concept, leaders develop a well-rounded group of key measures that address more than just the financial dimension of the business (for example, customer measures, human resource measures, process measures, and so on). A number of organizations have adopted the balanced scorecard, but many unfortunately continue to spend much more time and attention on the financial measures. Although many leaders conceptually agree with the premise of the balanced scorecard, the true commitment becomes apparent when the indicators drop. Those who don't truly believe in the concept will react much more quickly when the financial indicators fall than when the non-financial measures do. The objective of adopting a balanced system of metrics is to drive more focus on those aspects that drive the financial measures. Take care of these issues and the financial issues will take care of themselves. For example, focusing on and improving customer satisfaction will most likely be followed by an increase in sales revenues. On the other hand, if customer satisfaction measures decline, a drop in financial performance (lower sales revenues, earn-

Table 3.1   Causes of immeasurable but significant losses.

• Low employee morale	• Poor strategic planning
• Fear in the workplace	• Employee turnover
• Dissatisfied customers	• Poor supplier relations
• Lack of teamwork	• Too many suppliers

ings, and/or increased warranty expenses) can be expected to occur in the future.

Aren't the Numbers Important?

It is absolutely necessary to track and understand financial measures. At a high level, numbers provide a picture of how well the organization is achieving its purpose and whether or not it can continue to operate. Failing to monitor financial indicators and budgets can result in disastrous consequences for an organization.

Another important use of numbers is to solve problems and improve processes. Numbers provide the feedback necessary to understand whether a problem is the result of an isolated occurrence or a system level issue requiring management attention to resolve. Clear process-level metrics also help determine whether actions taken have resulted in the level of improvement desired.

The financial resources need to be managed in order to assure the capital is necessary to support the strategic direction of the business. Problems occur, however, when the financial measures become the main focus of the leaders rather than as a means to support the business and measure its success. It is also important to understand that the numbers do not tell the whole story.

Two problems with the number obsession exhibited by many managers today are a lack of understanding exactly what the numbers mean and the tendency to think of the numbers as the cause rather than the effect of company performance.

What Do the Numbers Mean?

Students at business schools spend a great deal of time in class learning about finance, including reporting, ratios, terms, and a variety of other finance and accounting measures. The result of this heavy emphasis on accounting is a large number of graduates entering the business world mistakenly thinking they can understand a business by looking at these measures.

On numerous occasions, I have witnessed executives from Fortune 500 companies who are visiting facilities of subsidiary companies making decisions and taking actions without ever leaving a meeting room. The decisions were made based solely on financial information presented during the meetings.

Although it's virtually impossible (nor desirable) for the leader of an organization to know everything that is happening within the operation, it is important to understand the overall system, including the general flow of information and material, the product or service produced, and how it all fits together. Key decisions should never be made without this basic understanding. When an executive visits a company without seeing the operation, he or she sends a strong message regarding its lack of importance. Whether it's a manufacturing or service organization, visiting it, and understanding how it works is the responsibility of every manager at every level in the company.

It is unfortunate that business today chooses leaders based more on their ability to analyze a spreadsheet or financial statements than on their ability to inspire people to improve systems and serve customers. Leaders who espouse to put customer needs above all else but, due to financial conditions, reduce the workforce to a level where the customer can't be effectively served, care more about the company's financial measures than its customers.

In the 1980s, when he was the CEO of Motorola, Robert Galvin decided to make quality improvement his main focus. To demonstrate his commitment to this initiative, he implemented a change in the format of his staff meetings by starting every meeting with a discussion of quality and improvement issues. To further drive his point, he would leave the meetings after the quality discussion ended, leaving the financial matters to the rest of his staff.

By leading the quality discussions and leaving the financial discussions to others, he demonstrated to the people at the company his commitment to quality and his confidence that financial improvement would result from the company's success with quality improvement.

A Matter of Cause and Effect

Financial results are the effect of running the business well. Too often, managers forget this simple concept and focus their efforts on the effect (financial results) instead of the causes (customers and the people and systems that serve them). One cannot improve a system by focusing on the effect. There is no leverage with which to act upon. It is necessary to clearly understand the causes that lead to the effects and use the causes as the leverage to improve the financial results. Bob Galvin understood this concept and applied it with great success during his tenure at Motorola. Throughout the years, managers at Toyota also understood the distinction between cause and effect, and achieved continual financial success by creating a model (and often copied) system of production. When traveling on Southwest Airlines, it becomes apparent that their focus is their people and customers, not financial measures; and no other major U. S. airline has come close to their level of success over the last several years. Managers at all of these companies understand their financial positions—they just don't overemphasize the measures and make them the main drivers of their businesses.

To successfully apply this concept, you have to truly believe that achieving your purpose will bring enough financial success to allow the business to operate and grow over the long term. Once you have this belief deeply rooted, you will focus on which causes result in the effect of achieving your purpose. Once identified, the causes that have the most leverage and are in the most need of improvement become the basis for the organization's strategic planning effort. Years ago, Toyota came to understand that their system of production was a major cause of their inability to compete with U. S. automakers. As a result, numerous innovations and continual improvements in their operation over the 50-plus years that followed led to solid and sustained financial success. Even during periods of recession when many other auto companies suffer, Toyota has been able to maintain solid financial returns.

Focus on the purpose is vital because it's the reason for the company's existence. Too often, managers become focused on the numbers, forget about the operation (that is, how the company serves its customers) and begin a never-ending cycle of cost-cutting.

Beware When You Compare

Another common misuse of numbers is for comparisons between operations. Given the proper environment, comparisons can be the basis for sharing of information between plants and increasing knowledge within the company. Trouble arises when the measures used for comparisons are tied to bonuses of the managers of the operations. Even when the measures are not tied to compensation, they can be misused, resulting in the creation of competition between operations. When competition arises, teamwork is destroyed, sharing ceases, and everyone loses.

An Example of Improper Comparisons

To attempt to gain control of their business, the management team of a manufacturing company with 14 facilities identified 25 metrics to be reported on a monthly basis. The data was collected by staff at the corporate office and reported to all plant managers (and others within the organization) on a graph comparing the performance of all facilities. To bring increased attention and focus to the metrics, the CEO discussed the results regularly in meetings with the plant managers and demanded explanations from the managers of the lower performing factories.

The immediate result of the initiative was to destroy the teamwork that existed between the plant managers. Prior to implementation of the program, there was a significant amount of orders shifted between the plants. If one plant were overscheduled, it would move work to another plant that had excess capacity. This practice helped each of the plants, the company, and the customer.

After the metrics program was established, however, the practice ended because of disagreements over intercompany pricing and credit for sales revenues. Visits by managers to other plants also diminished because of the increased level of competition that now existed.

In addition to the damage the program was doing to the plants, the comparisons were virtually useless to company management because the plants operated different equipment, served different markets, and often produced different products. To make matters worse, the graphs produced by the corporate office contained too much information for most people to comprehend. (See Figure 3.1 for an example of one of the graphs.)

The practice was stopped after one year.

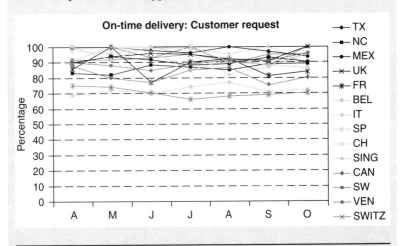

Figure 3.1 Plant comparison chart.

STOPPING THE MADNESS

In spite of what W. Edwards Deming and others tried to teach many years ago, the obsession managers have with financial measures has continued to worsen. Without a deeply held belief in the concept that the measurable characteristics of a business are not always accurate and don't provide information on the most important aspects of the organization, letting go of number obsession will be impossible.

Getting over the obsession is not easy because it is so deeply rooted in our society. A first step is for managers to learn how to understand what the numbers are telling them. Once the leaders realize how to better understand numbers, and how to understand and focus on true cause-and-effect relationships, transformation of the organization can begin.

An understanding of basic statistics and variation is necessary to gain knowledge from numbers. Fortunately, understanding and applying basic statistics does not require executives to be statistical experts. Basic statistical knowledge and learning to identify which numbers are truly important (and why) is an important step toward stopping organizational decline.

SPC for Management

Many companies (mostly in manufacturing) use statistical process control (SPC) within their operations to gain an understanding of their processes. Properly implemented, SPC can provide several benefits to the organization, including:

- Identifying whether variation in output is to be expected based on the design of the process, or the result of something special interfering with the operation

- Determining if the output of a process is stable enough and performing at a level where predictions can be made and inspection can be reduced or eliminated

- Understanding whether or not data from the process can be used to budget expected levels of output (including estimates of scrap and rework

- Giving direction for problem-solving efforts

These benefits are possible through the application of some basic statistical rules for understanding data. There are organizations in a variety of industries that do an excellent job of applying SPC within their operations, but completely ignore the same rules when looking at data in other parts of the company. On several occasions, I have worked with executives who surmised that a trend had developed after two or three data points, and demanded action in an attempt to improve the situation. Unfortunately, in each case, the action taken either had no effect at all or actually made the situation worse. Because managers often leave the implementation of SPC and the interpretation of results to an engineer or technician, they fail to gain an appreciation and clear understanding of the tool and its value.

When data is collected from a system and plotted on a line graph, an analysis of the resulting pattern can provide important information about

36   Chapter Three

the system. Using SPC (which involves applying some very basic statistical calculations), we can determine whether or not the system is predictable (sometimes referred to as *stable* or *in-control*). This is absolutely vital to understand how the system is operating, and how to facilitate improvement.

If all of the data points fall within the control limits (which are easily calculated and represent the expected level of variation in the system's results), about half of the points fall above and below the average, and there are no obvious patterns or trends, the system can most likely be considered stable.

Determining stability is important for several reasons. First of all, a stable system is predictable (within the control limits). For example, if the monthly gross margin percentage results for a company are plotted along with control limits and appear stable, it can be predicted that, without any major changes, the expected gross margin percentage for the coming year will fall within the control limits. In another example, if the wait time for a prescription at a pharmacy in a healthcare operation is charted and shown to be stable, the time to obtain a prescription in the future can be determined and planned accordingly.

Another advantage of understanding whether or not a system is stable deals with improving the system. If the system is stable, improvement must come from one or more major changes in the system. Understanding how to change a stable system requires analysis of the data collected over time to categorize and determine what elements most commonly interfere with improved results. Improving a stable system is often a long-term process, includes identifying and removing several causes of the problems identified, and usually requires management involvement to be successful.

On the other hand, improvement of an unstable system refers to identifying and eliminating the individual problems that are causing the system to be unstable. Improvement of the overall process cannot occur until it is made stable. If a system is unstable, improvement can come from analyzing the individual occurrences of instability (that is, the out-of-control points) and understanding what caused the problem(s). This can most likely be done by a person or team close to the system and improvements can often be implemented fairly quickly. Using the pharmacy example, if the wait time for prescriptions is deemed to be unacceptable, but the data shows the system to be stable, a redesign of the process is most likely necessary to make improvements. This may include a new or upgraded computer system, more resources, a physical move of the pharmacy, or a host of other options that require management attention. A team working on improving the process will need to identify and analyze all of the reasons for long wait times and look for common reasons in order to begin to improve the situation.

It should be noted that, as with the pharmacy example, a stable system does not necessarily produce acceptable results. A stable system is operating as designed, and its current design may not be capable of producing desired results. Stability is required, however, before improvements in capability can be made. Continuing with the example for prescription wait times in a hospital, if the process was not stable, the most a team would be able to do initially is to stabilize the process and make the wait times more predictable (which is obviously a benefit). Improving the process to consistently make the wait times shorter will not be able to be done until stability is obtained.

Figure 3.2 presents the results for warranty expenses as a percentage of sales for an electronics manufacturing company. Over a 12-month period, the company experienced warranty expenses ranging from about 0.7% of sales to 1% of sales. In addition to plotting the actual warranty values for each month, the graph includes a line for the average of the values (0.85%) and the control limits (0.55% and 1.15%). A quick review of the chart shows that the system is stable, which means that management of the company can expect warranty expenses for the coming year to be around 0.85% of sales, with monthly results to fall between 0.55% and 1.15% of sales. This information can be used to determine the budget for warranty expenses.

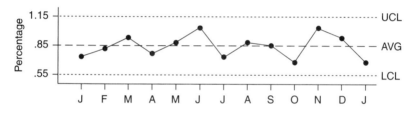

Figure 3.2 Warranty expenses.

Had the management team of the company in Figure 3.2 determined that 0.85% of sales was too high for warranty expenses, they would need to make significant changes to the systems that affect warranty costs to improve the situation. They should also expect that it will take time for the improvements to be implemented and take effect.

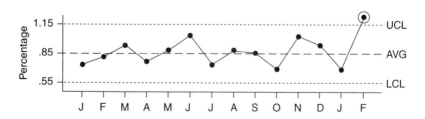

Figure 3.3 Warranty expenses with February result added.

Figure 3.3 shows the same chart as Figure 3.2 with February's result added. This chart shows that in February the system has become unstable, since the warranty expense for that month is above the upper control limit. Investigation of the problem involved an analysis of February's warranty claims to determine what had occurred. It was discovered that a supplier had mislabeled a shipment of resistors that was resulting in excessive field failures. Because this was not a normal occurrence (this was actually one of the company's best suppliers), it resulted in something outside of the system affecting its results. The problem was investigated and resolved and, even though it was expected that there would be additional warranty expenses in March due to the same problem, the system returned to a stable state.

It is important to keep in mind when looking at measures in this manner that unstable conditions require investigation, even if the result is on the beneficial side of the control limit. In the previous example, if warranty expenses fell below 0.55% of sales for a particular month, managers still need to investigate to discover what caused the improvement to occur. Remember that an unstable condition is caused by something outside of the system. If the cause of the condition is not determined, there would be little chance of standardizing the improvement so it will continue into the future. At best, the system will return to its normal operating state. At worst, the system will remain unstable, in effect leading to a loss of control of the system.

Figure 3.4 presents the on-time delivery result for the month of July for the largest factory of a manufacturing company. The newly appointed president of this company was very disappointed that the company delivered only 69% of its orders on time and demanded that the plant improve its delivery performance. He told the management team at the plant that he expected to see improvements by the end of

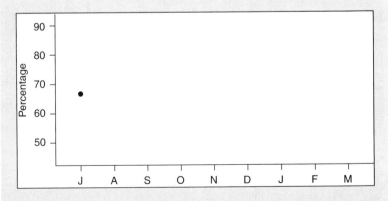

Figure 3.4 On-time delivery performance.

the following month. He also set a goal for the team of achieving on-time delivery performance of 95% by the end of the year. Factory managers assigned a team consisting of representatives from purchasing, production planning, and manufacturing to address the problem.

At the monthly meeting with corporate management, members of the team reported the steps that were taken to improve their ability to improve on-time delivery, as well as the actions implemented over the last few months to improve the system. When delivery performance for August was reported as 80%, the president was pleased and told the management team that he appreciated their efforts and expected the improvements to continue. When the results for September were reported as 64%, the president questioned the commitment of the team to satisfying the customer.

The leaders at the company in the preceding example did not understand the concept of variation with regard to performance measures. If they did, they would have approached the problem in a much different manner. The first step should have been to look at the results from previous months to determine if the system was stable. As is shown in Figure 3.5, even though delivery performance has been poor, the system has been very stable over the last 18 months. This means that the actions taken by the team actually had no effect on the system. The "good" result for August (80%) represented natural variation from the system as it is currently designed or resulted from the intense attention given to meeting delivery dates during the month by managers (something that could not continue into the future).

Using the information from Figure 3.5, the team should analyze the potential problems with delivering products on time and begin to look for commonalities among and frequency of the problems. This approach would lead the team to implement actions to eliminate the problem causes, resulting in improved delivery performance in the future. Because the data shows a stable system, improvement requires management involvement, requiring fundamental changes (for example, computer system modifications, plant layout improvements, supplier system improvements, and so on).

Regarding the goal of 95% on-time deliveries, the president should never have stated this until he knew whether the system was stable, and what its capability was. Because the upper control limit is 91%, it is virtually impossible for the factory to deliver 95% of its orders on time in any given month.

Once the management team (including the president) was trained in statistical methods, a high-level project was initiated to improve delivery

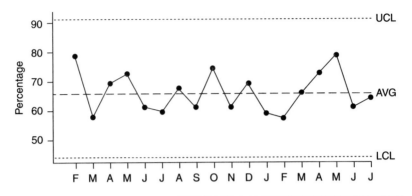

Figure 3.5 Historical on-time delivery performance.

performance. The project team included managers from the factory and the corporate office (since it was determined that the corporate office affected the plant's ability to deliver on time). After working on the project for several months, the system began to change, and delivery performance began to improve (see results in Figure 3.6). Delivery performance was improved (average increased to 86%) and the variation in results from month to month was reduced. The improvements made in the interactions between the corporate office and the factory also resulted in improvements in many of the company's other factories.

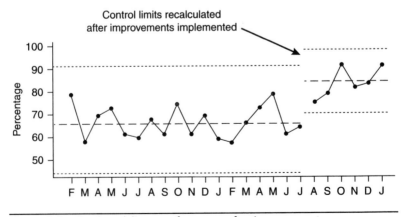

Figure 3.6 On-time delivery performance after improvement.

Another Example

The executive team in a hospital decided to set an objective to reduce billing errors. They determined that billing errors were resulting in increased costs for the hospital (including late payments and time spent dealing with insurance companies) and decreased patient satisfaction. They did not have any data on the extent of the problem, but decided to add billing errors to their key performance measures and identified an initiative to reduce the number of errors. No specific goal was determined because executive management understood that they did not know the extent of the problem and whether or not the system was stable.

Once data was collected and charted, it was determined that known billing errors were occurring on an average of 14.36% of bills. The system was very stable and control limits were running between 11.1% and 17.62%. This meant that reducing the percentage of errors would entail a fairly large effort and require management involvement.

A cross-functional team was set up to determine the causes of billing errors and begin to recommend improvements. Once they were able to classify three months of data regarding errors, they began to better understand the problem and better focus their efforts. The team was able to make significant improvements over the following year— reducing the average number of errors to 10.61%. Management forethought and understanding of statistics had enabled the team to be successful from the start of the project. They identified several classes of problems which were initiated in a number of areas throughout the hospital (for example, coding errors in the pharmacy, date errors in admissions, and so on). Because the entire management team took responsibility for the project, the team included representatives from virtually all functional areas, which made implementing improvements much easier.

Had the hospital management team approached the problem in a traditional manner, they would have assigned the project to an accounting manager and made it the manager's responsibility to improve the situation (possibly even tying a bonus to the result). There would not have been buy-in from other functional areas, resulting in little improvement and a whole lot of frustration.

You Don't Need To Be a Statistician

As mentioned earlier, applying SPC to management analysis does not require in-depth training in statistics. It does require a basic understanding

42 *Chapter Three*

of control charts, and how to take action based on the feedback provided in the charts.

There are a number of organizations in which executives will not accept any charts (including information related to sales, profits, inventory, and so on) without control limits. Managers in organizations following this practice make more informed decisions and waste less time discussing, analyzing and misinterpreting data.

This book is not intended to be a book on SPC. Appendix B presents more detailed information regarding SPC. There are also many books and software packages that provide much more in-depth explanations on statistical theory, formulas, and application methods on the subject. Two excellent references on the subject include *Understanding Statistical Process Control* by Donald Wheeler (SPC Press, 1992) which covers the technical aspects of implementation and use of SPC, and *Fourth Generation Management* (McGraw-Hill Companies, 1994) by Brian Joiner provides several examples of management applications of SPC.

What About Financial Targets?

Curing an obsession with numbers may mean letting go of some very deeply rooted beliefs. One widely held belief deals with earnings forecasts. In an effort to appease financial analysts, U. S. companies have somehow been led to believe that they need to publish earnings forecasts. If the experts believe in the forecasts, the stock price may rise. At the end of the quarter or year, however, if earnings fall short of the forecast, the stock price falls. Even if the company meets or beats its forecast, its stock price may still fall if analysts believe the company should have done better. Unfortunately, the whole process is a game that results in a lot of effort with little or no value.

There are two major drawbacks to the practice of providing earnings forecasts to financial markets. First, the estimates are always incorrect. Second, the estimates take the focus of management away from important activities (like improving the business and delighting customers), and toward earnings and other financial activities (that is, the *effect* instead of the *cause*). It is very common for divisions to project their earnings, only to have them rejected and inflated by parent company management. In some companies, however, management recognized the problems with earnings estimates and have stopped the practice. Coca-Cola, Berkshire-Hathaway, Gillette, and the Washington Post are four well-known companies that have made the decision to not publish earnings estimates.

When Coca-Cola announced that it was ceasing to release earnings forecasts, it justified the move by stating that such forecasts drew attention away from its efforts to build a successful business in the long run.[3]

IDENTIFYING NUMBER OBSESSION

It is usually very easy to identify from the inside whether an organization in which you work is number obsessed. Looking for clues in the things that get management attention and drive management action is a good way to start. How frequently are drastic cost cutting directives initiated and what is the usual response to these directives? If the usual response is layoffs, pay cuts, or other actions that negatively impact employees or customers, odds are fairly good that the company is number obsessed.

Another characteristic of number-obsessed organizations is the ratio of financial professionals to technical professionals. The ratio should be heavily weighted toward jobs related directly to the product or service offered by the company. If it is not, be wary of company management's focus.

Another clear sign of number obsession is the practice of starting high-level meetings with financial measures. If financial measures are always first or regularly dominate the conversations, management is number obsessed. Number-obsessed managers also may know the dollar value of shipments at a given point in time, but don't seem to care about the company's on-time delivery performance to its customers.

If you're looking for a job, and want to avoid a numbers-obsessed organization, there are several questions you can ask that will help in your search. First of all, ask about the company's key metrics. If they are all, or heavily weighted toward, financial measures, it is probably a numbers-obsessed organization. Ask about the non-financial measures like customer satisfaction, on-time delivery, or employee satisfaction, and listen carefully to the responses to discover whether or not these things get the level of attention that financial measures do.

In addition to the non-financial measures, inquire about some of the areas that can cost the company a great deal of money but can't be measured, like fear in the workplace or lack of teamwork among employees. Although there is virtually no way to accurately measure the costs of these things, you can get an idea of whether or not management is concerned about them and if they are taking action to make improvements.

When deciding whether or not to invest money in a company, read through the company's annual report to see how focused the CEO and/or Chairman of the Board appear to be on financial matters. If the message appears to emphasize growth, acquisitions, stock price (or shareholder value), and similar topics, more than quality, customer satisfaction, and core business strengths, the company is probably financially focused.

In addition to the annual report, check published customer satisfaction ratings to determine if the company serves its customers well. Other sources of information about the company's focus on numbers instead of its business

44 *Chapter Three*

include newspaper and Internet articles. Newspaper and magazine articles can be a valuable resource for people to use before investing money in companies. If the company seems to have frequent job cuts and plant closings in response to economic pressures, its management may care more about numbers than its employees or its customers. There are many examples of large organizations that have weathered tough economic times without laying off workers (for example, Hewlett-Packard in the early 1990s, Southwest Airlines after the September 11, 2001 attacks, RyanAir, Nucor Steel, and Toyota which has not had a layoff since 1949). The immediate numbers are obviously not the primary concern of the management in these companies.

SUMMARY

The danger with a numbers obsession is the tendency to think that the numbers are the means *and* the end, and to forget about the things that are truly important to the business. Focusing too heavily on the numbers also leads to short-term thinking. The numbers are nothing more than an indication (though not always an accurate indication) of how well the business is managed.

Leading and building the health of an organization is much more difficult than working with numbers. If it weren't, there would be many more effective leaders and we wouldn't need to pay high salaries to CEOs. Necessary elements of leadership include: frequent visits to the operation to learn, understand, and talk with the people doing the work; regular dialogue with customers and suppliers to better understand the issues they face; continual efforts to develop the talents and skills of the people within the organization; clear and consistent communication of the purpose of the organization; and effective long-term planning.

Numbers can be managed, but organizations must be led.

NOTES

[1] Kelleher, Herb. 1997. "A Culture of Commitment." *Leader to Leader,* 4/Spring.

[2] Kaplan, Robert S., and David P. Norton. 1992. "The Balanced Scorecard: Measures that Drive Performance." *Harvard Business Review,* January 1.

[3] Weber, Harry R. 2002. "Coke to Stop Offering Quarterly or Annual Earnings Forecasts." Associated Press, December 14.

4

Supplier Squeezing

"An essential to being a world-class quality company
is to be a world-class customer."
—Robert Galvin[1]

> **Definition**
>
> *Management does not value the relationship with suppliers and focuses procurement efforts on reducing the price of incoming products and services instead of working toward a long-term mutually beneficial relationship to improve quality, cost, and delivery.*

The third sign of organizational decline involves the way in which organizations deal with their suppliers. Companies that base a significant portion of their relationship on price are doomed to receive poor incoming materials or services from their suppliers, which leads to a host of problems including increased cycle times, more inventory, a higher number of production problems, higher warranty expenses, higher costs, and dissatisfied customers.

It is not surprising that those companies that practice supplier squeezing are also the ones that are number obsessed. And if the management of these companies truly understood numbers, they would realize that supplier squeezing actually increases total costs for the company when compared to developing and improving the overall relationship with the supplier.

CONSIDERING TOTAL COST

The purchase price is only one of many components of the total cost incurred by a company when it purchases materials or services. The fact that

46   *Chapter Four*

it's the easiest to measure probably explains why it is usually the only component considered when evaluating a supplier. Ease of measure, however, has absolutely nothing to do with organizational success. Table 4.1 provides an actual example of an organization that chose a supplier based solely on purchase price and ended up incurring large additional costs as a result.

The company in Table 4.1 was evaluating three potential sources for steel castings. Because all three suppliers had done business with the company in the past, performance data was available for each.

Supplier A was a local foundry that was located within 10 miles of the customer's manufacturing facility and had supplied the company with castings for the previous 20-plus years. Supplier B's foundry was located about 500 miles from the customer, and Supplier C was overseas, producing castings in another country.

Based on price alone, Supplier C was the easy choice, saving the company $22 per casting compared to Supplier A, and $20 when compared to Supplier B. Due to the low reject rate, however, castings from Supplier A would not require inspection when received. Suppliers B and C would require a certain level of inspection to screen out the defective castings. The cost of inspection to the company would increase the cost of castings from Supplier B by $7, and Supplier C by $17.

To understand the impact of quality, however, it's important to look at more than the acceptance or rejection rates of the parts it receives. Even

Table 4.1   Example of total cost analysis for a supplier.

	Supplier A	Supplier B	Supplier C
Price	$42	$40	$20
Inspection costs	$0	$7	$17
Variation–added hrs	0.0	0.1	0.2
–added costs	$0	$4	$8
Reject rate	.01%	5%	12%
On-time delivery (%)	94%	72%	79%
Leadtime–days	8	12	30
Extra inventory costs	$1	$1.50	$5
Design support	Yes	No	No
Daily delivery	Yes	Yes	No
Total costs	$43	$52.50	$50

when products are produced within specification (for example, within a given tolerance range), the amount of variation within products and between the products can affect costs. Increased amount of variation can result in increased machining and/or assembly time due to extra handling required to make the parts fit together. Excessive variation can also result in difficulties for the customer, including extra wear and problems retrofitting spare parts.

Based on past experience, the company determined that Supplier A had the least amount of variation in products received. The increased amount of variation from Suppliers B and C would result in increased machining and assembly times of 6 minutes for B's castings, and 12 minutes for C's castings (which costs the company $4 and $8, respectively).

The historical on-time delivery performance from Supplier A is 95%, Supplier B is 72%, and Supplier C is 79%. When coupled with the normal lead times of eight days from Supplier A, 12 days from Supplier B, and 30 days from Supplier C, this results in the need to order larger quantities of material from each supplier which, when calculated, means an extra inventory costs of $1 for castings from Supplier A, $1.50 from Supplier B, and $5 from Supplier C.

Some of the non-calculable benefits of Supplier A include design support to help the company develop castings that are easier to produce, cost less, and are easier to handle, and daily deliveries of castings to keep the company's inventory costs down (Supplier B had also committed to daily deliveries).

As a result of a comparison of the criteria presented in Table 4.1, the castings from each supplier, the best choice would be Supplier A, whose cost per casting would be $43. The second lowest cost castings came from Supplier C (at $50 per casting), and Supplier B resulted in the highest costs, at $52.50 per casting.

Not surprisingly, Supplier C was chosen, based on the purchase price of $20 per casting, and Supplier B was selected to be a backup. This decision was made because, at the time, there was no effort or initiative to calculate the total cost of dealing with the suppliers. Many of the people within the company (especially within the manufacturing areas) felt that Supplier A was the best supplier but did not have the data to back up their opinions. The Purchasing Manager, who was measured on keeping purchase price down, made the decision even though he also thought Supplier A was the best for the company.

The result for the company was that they gave away $7 for every casting they used because it cost $50 for every casting they purchased from Supplier C, versus $43 for each casting purchased from Supplier A. And since this figure does not include the factors that cannot be measured including a lack of design support, delivery delays to customers because of

48   Chapter Four

Table 4.2   Total cost of purchased materials.

Total costs = P + I + F + O

Where;

P = Purchase price

I = Cost of inspection

F = Failure costs (cost to the company if problems are found internally, plus warranty costs if found externally by the customer)

O = Other costs:
- On-time delivery % (adding to inventory costs)
- Lead time (adding to inventory costs)
- Product/material variation (additional machining/assembly time)
- Order quantities required (adding to inventory costs)
- Design support
- Continual improvement philosophy
- Payment terms

quality or delivery problems from Supplier C, and damage to the relationship with Supplier A (which affects the other products Supplier A provides), the loss resulting from this decision is even higher.

Another factor that made the decision to purchase from Supplier C a poor one for the company was the fact that Supplier A had been actively practicing a continual improvement process for several years, which undoubtedly would have led to reductions in the costs in the future.

Although Table 4.1 relates to a manufacturing organization, the same concept applies to service organizations. The purchase of supplies and services result in total costs to the organization that is far in excess of the purchase price.

Table 4.2 presents some of the costs related to purchased goods and services. Depending on the type of product or service purchased, as well as other company-specific circumstances, some of these costs are higher than others. Looking at the number of elements of the total cost of procurement, one has to question the practice of focusing solely on price and payment terms.

For non-manufacturing organizations, Table 4.3 presents some of the costs related to the purchase of supplies and items for resale. Although this list is far from exhaustive, it gives enough information so that the cost of purchased supplies is much higher than what is merely reflected in the purchase price.

Table 4.3 Costs associated with purchase of supplies.

The costs of purchasing supplies and products for resale include any or all of the following:

1. *Purchase price:* The price reflected on the invoice.

2. *Failure costs:* The costs associated with problems discovered in-house (e.g., surgical kits with missing components, plasticware kits with defective knives, etc.), as well as problems found by the customer.

3. *Lead time:* The costs of carrying extra inventory due to the lead time necessary to place orders and replenish stock, and the ability of the supplier to respond quickly to unforeseen demand.

4. *Payment terms:* The date on which payment is due for supplies purchased.

5. *Delivery performance:* The reliability of delivery dates. The more unreliable a supplier is on meeting delivery commitments, the more inventory needs to be carried to prevent outages.

6. *Ability/willingness to customize:* The more willing and able the supplier is to customize, the better the possibility for increased efficiency and customer satisfaction. As an example, special packaging to make it easier and quicker to use the supplies.

7. *Minimum order quantities:* The lower the minimum order quantities required by the supplier, the less inventory that needs to be held resulting in lower inventory costs.

8. *Continual improvement philosophy:* Suppliers that continually strive to improve tend to provide lower costs and/or better quality to its customers.

SUPPLIER TURNOVER

Organizations that change suppliers often in order to lower or contain material costs usually have the highest total costs and the most problems with incoming material. Recently, the executive staff at a Fortune 200 company issued a directive to its subsidiary division purchasing managers to turn over 50 percent of their suppliers every three years. It is unfortunate that the people in charge of developing the corporate purchasing strategy for the company do not understand purchasing management. It is policies like this that build distrust between supplier and customer (as well as between purchasing and manufacturing), a situation where everyone loses.

If the objective of the purchasing system is to reduce the total cost to the company, there needs to be continual development and improvement of key suppliers, which can only occur through long-term relationships. A supplier

50 *Chapter Four*

that does not feel like a long-term relationship will develop with a customer will most likely not make investments in new and improved machinery and equipment for that customer's products or services. They also will not be able to take the time necessary to learn about the customer's business well enough to improve the level of service provided. The key is understanding that suppliers are a part of your organization (that is, your system). And when your suppliers suffer, you suffer.

A goal of turning over suppliers is similar to a goal of turning over employees. Most would agree that turning over machinists, engineers, and others within an organization is damaging to the company. Yet an equally damaging situation occurs whenever a company changes suppliers.

A Holistic Approach to Procurement

Those who consider the job of supply managers to be purely cost containment lack a holistic, or systems, perspective of the organization. *Systems thinking* is a concept that aims at assuring success of the system as a whole instead of the individual components. A person who thinks and acts with the system in mind realizes that the objective of the components is to contribute to the success of the system.

One of the most important aspects of systems thinking is the realization that nothing in an organization is done that doesn't affect one or more other parts of the organization. When material is purchased, it can affect people in receiving, inspection, manufacturing, testing, accounting, and shipping, as well as the end customer. Focusing solely on price ignores the effect the incoming material has on the other parts of the organization.

W. Edwards Deming introduced the concept of systems thinking in business to the Japanese in 1950, which gave them a new way of looking at an organization. He later wrote about the importance for leaders to appreciate systems in his book, *The New Economics*[2]. Peter Senge refers to systems thinking as the *fifth discipline*, and explores the subject in great depth in his book, *The Fifth Discipline—The Art and Practice of the Learning Organization*[3]. It is unfortunate that the subject has been published in these two highly successful books but is still misunderstood and ignored by so many leaders.

A systems approach to supply management would focus on assuring the lowest *total* cost for incoming material, which includes much more than price. Table 4.2 presents a general formula for total cost. The formula is basic, but provides the framework for measuring how suppliers are contributing to the organization's success.

It is not necessary to measure every component of total cost to select and work with suppliers. In fact, some of the components cannot be effectively measured. The important point of total cost analysis is to realize that it includes much more than price, and that forcing purchasing managers to focus only on price usually leads to poor decisions and higher total costs for the company. The key is to think in total cost terms.

Another aspect of systems thinking is the notion that suppliers need to be successful for the customer to be successful. Squeezing suppliers on price can lead to a host of quality problems that result from the supplier's efforts to cut costs in order to remain profitable. The situation gets worse when the supplier squeezes its suppliers and the problems work their way up the supply chain.

If your suppliers suffer, your organization will also suffer. Organizations rarely practice as if they believe this concept. One vivid example of taking care of suppliers comes from the Nissan Corporation[4]. In the early 1950s, Nissan was in serious financial trouble and facing a potentially long-term labor strike. In order to prepare for the strike, the company was able to arrange loans from the Industrial Bank of Japan. Part of the loan was for Nissan's suppliers, to help them survive what was expected to be a long-term work stoppage. Management at Nissan during the time understood the importance of their suppliers in their own future success (and, in fact, survival). There aren't many companies today that would take the same actions to help their suppliers.

As a part of your system, suppliers are very similar to your own employees. They directly contribute to your ability to serve customers and be successful by providing materials, products, and services in much the same way as people internal to the organization. When considered in this manner, one has to ask whether or not it makes sense with your own employees to:

- Demand continual reductions in salaries and wages

- Require delays in issuing paychecks as a condition of continued employment

- Consider employee turnover to be a good thing for the organization

- Bring in new people regularly in an attempt to bid down employee pay

As ridiculous as these ideas sound from an employee-relations standpoint, many companies do these things everyday with their suppliers.

[*For more on systems-related issues, refer to warning sign 6: Operational Fragmentation.*]

When the Supplier Suffers, the Customer Suffers

Those who don't understand or practice systems thinking often feel like the only way they can win in a relationship with suppliers is when the supplier

52   Chapter Four

loses. Today's business world is unfortunately overloaded with constant reminders of this type of thinking.

A large U. S.-based multi-division manufacturer of diversified products recently implemented a policy that targets delaying payments to suppliers for 90-plus days after receiving the products or services. The company's corporate purchasing group has spent considerable time and money marketing this policy to their purchasing teams (they even gave it a clever mnemonic and slogan to make it easier to remember), and measures each division's progress in moving suppliers into this program. When corporate executives visit the subsidiaries, they always request that division management make a presentation regarding their progress in implementation of the directive.

This initiative has led to damage in the relationship between the divisions and their suppliers, some of whom have actually severed ties with the company. It's a sad state for a company when its suppliers, in effect, fire them. Other suppliers have refused the new payment terms, which has forced the division purchasing teams to spend time developing explanations for the corporate staff, and setting up special payment terms for the suppliers, which adds complexity to the company's accounts payable team because of special handling for certain suppliers. The result has been a loss of time and damage to the relationships with suppliers, the cost of which has more than offset the savings achieved by delaying payments. In one instance, a supplier of one of the divisions implemented its own policy requiring a division to prepay for products it ordered. The irony of this situation was that the supplier was, in fact, another division of the same parent company.

A policy of delaying payments to suppliers is another example of managing by numbers. Executives feel like they are saving money for the company by holding on to cash longer. Once again, however, the non-measurable costs (as shown in Table 4.4) are ignored.

Who's the Customer?

The main objective of purchasing professionals today is to serve those who use the materials and services they purchase. This is a very basic notion, but one that cannot be understood without a systems perspective to purchasing.

Not long ago, I was talking with a purchasing agent in a manufacturing company about the products that she purchased. One of the main products she handled was steel pipe, which was used by a manufacturing operation located in the same complex as her office, but in a different building. During our discussion, she told me that in the eight years she had been purchasing the pipe, she had never gone out to the shop floor to find out what the people in the manufacturing process thought about the pipe that she pur-

Supplier Squeezing 53

Table 4.4 Losses to a company resulting from delaying payments to a supplier.

1. Damaged relationship with the supplier

2. Supplier unable to invest in new machinery and equipment

3. Short-term cost cutting measures by the supplier, including:
   −Reductions in maintenance of equipment
   −Reductions in training of workers
   −Layoffs and/or increased employee turnover

4. Late deliveries / lengthened leadtimes

5. Poor quality parts, materials and services

6. Increased supplier turnover, resulting in time and cost associated with search for new suppliers

7. Pressure on sub-tier suppliers resulting in similar problems down the supply chain

chased for them to use. She was so accustomed to thinking of the purchasing manager as her customer that she had focused her entire efforts on reducing the price of pipe and making the purchasing manager happy. As we talked about whom her true customer was, it was as if she had never even considered the users of the pipe.

Unfortunately, this mode of thinking is not confined solely to the purchasing profession. In most companies, workers think of the boss as the main customer instead of the person(s) using the product or service they produce. This leads to a heavy focus on pleasing the boss, whether or not it negatively affects the customer. For those in a support role (for example, purchasing), the customer is usually someone inside the organization who is working on the product or service that serves the external customer.

If management thinks that the main objective of purchasing is to keep the price of purchased materials down, then that is where the people doing the buying will focus their efforts. The needs of manufacturing and/or the final customer may be considered, but only if it doesn't negatively affect the price.

In another example, a purchasing manager for a hospital system implemented a measurement system for purchasing agents to measure the degree to which the agent was able to reduce the costs of supplies and services purchased in their areas of responsibility. The measurement system included a sophisticated formula that included hospital revenues, the rate of inflation, and historical purchase costs. Nowhere in the evaluation was the satisfaction of those who used the products and services taken into

54 Chapter Four

account. As a result, purchasing agents had less time available to talk with those who requisitioned the purchase because of the time they spent looking for new lower-cost sources of supply or working down the price from existing suppliers. New requisition and justification forms were implemented that further separated the agents from their internal customers. The program resulted in reducing the price of incoming materials and services by 7 percent in the first year but was abandoned after managers in the individual hospitals revolted against the purchasing department because of the problems caused by the policy. Although the total cost of the program was never calculated, it was fairly well accepted that the increase was far greater than the 7 percent saved in purchase price. The measurement was dropped, purchasing was decentralized, and internal satisfaction increased. Perhaps the people who were the happiest with dropping the program were the purchasing agents, who knew they were causing damage for the organization.

Procurement and the Internet

The Internet has great potential for improving the relationship between suppliers and customers. Customers and suppliers can now exchange information quickly and inexpensively to enable them both to become more successful. It is unfortunate that in many instances the impact of the Internet on purchasing has been just the opposite.

Those who do not understand the importance of developing long-term relationships with suppliers have used the Internet to completely change the way in which industrial buyers and sellers deal with each other. Sophisticated software packages have been developed to allow organizations to post their needs on a website so potential buyers can submit their price for the products posted. These packages allow the buyer to watch the website like a ticker tape as suppliers attempt to outbid each other in an eBay-type auction for the business. While the bidding process is occurring, there is excitement among the purchasing people as suppliers post lower and lower prices for the product or service listed. Suppliers can see what other companies are bidding (although company names are kept confidential) and decide whether or not to lower their price as the bidding continues.

This type of online system allows companies to change suppliers for every purchase, if they so desire. There is usually no effort to determine the quality philosophy or systems in place at the supplier. The objective of the system is to drive down the price of the goods purchased with no regard to the relationship between buyer and seller. Although many companies plan to verify the quality systems of the lowest bidder after the process is completed, price is still used as the main factor for decision-making.

In some instances, companies will put a purchased component out for an online bid just to force their current supplier to lower their price. Even though they have no intention of changing suppliers, they will use the process to squeeze the supplier for a lower price. The damage to the relationship caused by this practice, although not directly measurable, is significant. When the customer shows no concern for the supplier's success, the supplier will return the favor by showing no concern for the customer.

Many companies that use Internet-based bidding systems set goals for their purchasing departments that reward (or punish) the buyers based on the number of products converted to the online bidding process. As is usually the case, this interferes with the purchasing professional's ability to develop suppliers and reduce the total cost of purchased items.

Recently, a medium-sized manufacturing company held a supplier forum for its 50 largest suppliers. The day began with presentations by the president of the company and the vice president of procurement regarding how committed the company was to developing long-term relationships with suppliers, with the objective of providing the highest quality products to its customers. Later in the day, the company made a presentation about the online bidding system that it was planning to use for at least 25% of its business in the coming year. The mixed messages given to the suppliers made them realize that, although the company talked about quality, continual improvement, and long-term relationships, they were mostly interested in price. This resulted in a huge loss of credibility by the company.

WHAT IS THE OBJECTIVE OF PROCUREMENT?

The overriding objective of purchasing is to reduce the total cost of incoming materials. Conceptually, the objective is obvious, but implementation of the concept is where most purchasing professionals fail.

Although attempting to calculate the total cost of a purchase may be a difficult process that could very well cost more than the material itself, there are some steps that can be taken that are well aligned with the concept and, if done effectively, would result in lowering the total cost of purchased material, even without attempting to measure.

Reducing Supplier Base

The first thing that purchasing people can focus on is reducing the supplier base. The more suppliers a company has, the more variation in incoming material and services they will experience, leading to a host of potential problems including poorer quality of the final product, quicker wear of moving parts, and increased times for handling and assembly times. Companies with large supplier bases also miss out on the continual improvements in quality, cost, and product cycle times that a close relationship with a supplier can bring.

56   Chapter Four

One organization I worked with in the past had over one thousand active suppliers. The most disturbing fact about the situation is that the company itself had less than nine hundred employees. This means that there was more than one supplier for every employee in the company. There is no possible way that anyone had the time to work with suppliers to improve the quality of incoming material.

There should be no more than one supplier per type of purchased product or service. Concerns about whether this practice puts the company at risk if the supplier can't deliver won't be valid if the process is handled correctly. If a company develops a relationship with a supplier and works with it as a partner to improve its processes, it will know whether or not a potential problem exists. Assigning all of your company's business for a particular product or service to a single supplier without taking the time to understand the supplier's processes and business philosophy, however, can be a very dangerous practice.

Problems occur, however, when purchasing managers reduce their supplier base before working with and developing suppliers. Business philosophy, desire for and commitment to improvement, and quality system effectiveness are a few of the aspects that need to be considered when selecting suppliers for a product or service. Too often, price or some other aspect is used, which virtually always leads to problems for the company.

When reducing the supplier base, the focus initially should be on the suppliers of critical products or services to the company. This way, those suppliers that have the most significant effect on the business will initially receive the most attention.

Satisfying Internal Customers

When developing suppliers to reduce the total cost of incoming material, it is vital to work with those who are most affected by the materials or services purchased. Project teams consisting of manufacturing, engineering, quality, and representatives from any other affected area can greatly improve the process for evaluating and developing suppliers. Inviting the supplier to your facility to see how the products or services they provide are used, and how it affects those inside of the organization and the end user, can also yield huge benefits for your organization.

Continual Improvement in Purchased Products

As mentioned earlier, one of the key aspects of choosing a supplier is the philosophy of the supplier organization's management with regard to continual improvement. If the organization does not have the continual improvement philosophy engrained within its culture, it will most likely not be able to *flip a switch* and begin improvement just because you asked them to do so. Too often, companies put up a façade of an active process because they have been forced by customers to implement the philosophy. Unless the drive for continual improvement comes from inside the organization, improvements made will probably be more cosmetic in nature rather than long term and sustainable.

The purchasing professional must learn how the supplier feels about continual improvement. This includes the type of training the supplier has provided to teach its people about the continual improvement process and the level of success the company has had in improving its processes.

Improvement should be able to be demonstrated in terms of gains in quality, cost, and delivery (including on-time delivery performance and overall product cycle times). It will be fairly evident whether or not the company has truly made gains in these areas from a structured approach to resolving problems and improving processes by looking at the results of the process. Organizations that are successful in continually improving their processes usually have no trouble demonstrating results including reduced cycle times, lower scrap and/or rework expenses, or any other type of key improvement. In fact, most who follow the practice are proud of their accomplishments and are eager to share the results.

If the purchasing department focuses on the aforementioned areas (reducing the supplier base, using internal customer feedback and expertise to develop suppliers, and gaining an understanding of supplier's continual improvement philosophy), it will most likely meet its objective of reducing the total cost of incoming material. Those who attempt to measure or evaluate the purchasing system should also be looking at these things rather than focusing solely on purchase price.

BEING A GREAT CUSTOMER

When companies have problems with suppliers, the tendency is to exert a great deal of pressure on the suppliers to improve. In many instances, however, the problems are self-inflicted, caused more by the company than the supplier. Unrealistic due dates, incomplete or conflicting product information, and poor designs are just a few of the problems that companies cause for suppliers. And these problems eventually come back to the company in the form of poor quality products and services from the supplier. Unfortunately, these same companies never seem to make the connection between how they deal with their suppliers and the quality of the products and services they receive in return. They often further damage the relationship by demanding that the supplier take action to resolve the problems that they have caused themselves.

58   *Chapter Four*

There are a few companies, however, that conduct surveys of their suppliers to find out how easy of a customer they are with which to do business and what kind of things they can do to improve. Openly receiving and acting on feedback from suppliers can result in significant improvements in the quality of purchased goods. Taking this approach with suppliers, however, requires an open mind and a genuine desire to improve. Because of a fear of losing business, some suppliers will not provide honest feedback to a customer.

MOST UNDERSTAND, SO WHAT'S THE PROBLEM?

I have presented the information in this chapter to organizations and at meetings of purchasing professionals on several occasions, and have always found the material to be well received by those in attendance. These concepts are not difficult to grasp and are even included within the body of knowledge in the Certified Purchasing Manager certification from the Institute for Supply Management. Why, then, is there a problem in implementing the concept in so many organizations?

Once again, it comes down to the philosophy and actions of management. If management of the organization does not understand the role of purchasing and supplier development in the success of the organization, they will tamper with the purchasing system and develop initiatives and measures that focus on the simplest aspects of procurement: price and payment terms. As mentioned throughout this chapter, a heavy focus on price by the management of an organization leads to losses for the customer, the supplier, and interferes with the development of the people in the purchasing department. It is for this reason that squeezing suppliers is a clear sign that the organization is in decline.

Another sign of squeezing suppliers is the practice of enlisting multiple suppliers for single products or services purchased. It is not practical to work with and develop suppliers to continually improve the quality and lead time of incoming materials if a multiple supplier strategy exists.

IDENTIFYING SUPPLIER SQUEEZING

As with the other warning signs, identifying it from inside of the organization is a fairly easy task. Look at what the purchasing department employees focus on the most. If you are in a position that uses materials or services from suppliers, have you ever been approached by the person who places the order about the quality of the material or service? If price reductions, material cost containment, or lengthening the payment terms to suppliers are discussed in meetings and presentations to management more than development and improvement of suppliers, you can feel fairly confident that the organization is squeezing suppliers. Another sign of squeezing suppliers is the practice of enlisting multiple suppliers for single products or services purchased. It is not practical to work with and develop suppliers to continually improve the quality and lead time of incoming material if a multiple supplier strategy exists.

If you are interviewing for a job with a company, you can use the opportunity to ask questions to determine if the company squeezes suppliers. Ask about the size of the supplier base. If it is large compared to the size of the organization (or large compared to the size of the purchasing department), it means that the company doesn't actively manage its suppliers. Since it is difficult to ascertain if the supplier base is too large for the type of company you are interviewing with, ask about the company's philosophy on sole sources for a particular type of product or service.

Ask the people you meet during the interviewing process what the most important issue is regarding suppliers. If you don't receive consistent answers, or there is an emphasis on price containment, dig a little deeper to understand if supplier squeezing exists. You should become more concerned if you find that those using the materials (for example, manufacturing areas) express the need to improve quality, while the purchasing people focus on price reductions.

You can also inquire about how the company develops suppliers. Does it focus on quality, delivery, and total cost? Does the supplier development process involve people from areas other than purchasing, or do visits to suppliers usually consist of a purchasing agent only, who attempts to represent all functional areas.

Identifying the existence of supplier squeezing is much more difficult for a potential investor. As with the other warning signs, the annual report is usually a good place to start. It is usually a good sign if the CEO or Chairman of the Board's message includes a statement regarding the importance of suppliers to the company.

Another source of information includes magazine and newspaper articles. If any of the articles available present any information on the company's suppliers, look for clues on how they consider the relationship. Stories of battles between a company and one or more of its suppliers are in the news fairly regularly. Reading these articles can provide a fairly good insight into how the company values the relationship and treats its suppliers. As an example, the newspapers recently reported a study about suppliers of a large company experiencing financial troubles. The story stated that 85% of this company's suppliers surveyed reported a poor working relationship with the company, compared to only 3% who claimed a good or very good working relationship. This situation is obviously a clear sign that the company does not value its relationships with its suppliers.

Talking with people in the industry can also provide information. There are some companies that have strong reputations (good and bad) within particular industries on their dealings with suppliers. Within the automotive industry, there are a few companies that are well known for having perfected the art of squeezing suppliers, sometimes to the point of forcing suppliers into bankruptcy.

Once you learn whether or not an organization squeezes suppliers, you can determine if you should avoid the company or work within it to transform its practices and remove the cause of the warning sign.

SUMMARY

The key to optimizing the system for purchasing materials and suppliers is to understand the total cost implications. Even if attempts to understand total cost are not completely accurate, there will be enough information to realize the impact of implementing a strategy and making decisions. Total cost is a concept that can align everyone in the organization, reduce conflict, and improve customer satisfaction and company performance.

NOTES

[1] Motorola, Inc. 1991. "The Eleven Welcome Heresies of Quality." *Quality Forum Newsletter,* I:II.

[2] Deming, W. Edwards. 1994. *The New Economics for Industry, Government, Education.* Cambridge, MA: MIT Press.

[3] Senge, Peter. 1990. *The Fifth Discipline: The Art and Practice of the Learning Organization.* New York: Doubleday.

[4] Halberstam, David. 1986. *The Reckoning.* New York: Avon Books.

5

Undervalued Employees

Trust is a small word with huge implications for how you manage your company and how employees feel about working there.
—Brian Joiner[1]

> **Definition**
>
> *A situation where leaders do not place a high value on employees. Layoffs are common, fear is prevalent, and there is very little leadership development within the organization. Attempts are made to measure employee performance without taking into account non-measurable contributions.*

Are your employees proud to be a part of your organization? Determining how happy and proud the employees are is one of the quickest ways to assess organizational health. Quite simply, for those companies that consider employees as expenses, a low degree of dedication and loyalty from the employees generally exists, and any success achieved is usually short-lived. On the other hand, companies that are known for valuing their workers and truly treating them as assets, like Toyota, RyanAir, Nucor Steel, and Southwest Airlines, have demonstrated long-term success, even during troubled times. Understanding the benefits of a happy and proud workforce is a simple concept but one that is unfortunately rarely practiced (Figure 5.1).

The plethora of overused clichés, such as *employees are our most important asset,* demonstrate that this concept is not new to the business world. As is usually the case, however, it is actions rather than words that demonstrate one's true beliefs. And the actions of Western business executives over the last

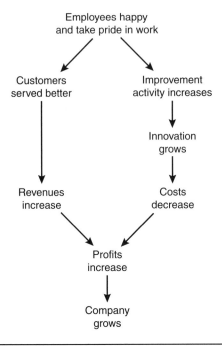

Figure 5.1 Success and happy employees.

10–20 years have shown that employees are expenses that are among the first to be cut when revenues fall.

CUTTING ASSETS TO IMPROVE PROFIT

When it appears that cost cutting is necessary, management must decide whether to reduce assets or expenses. Those who resort to employee layoffs obviously consider employees as expenses, because it is not logical to throw away assets in response to a downturn in business. This is unfortunate because not only are employees assets to the organization, but also they are an asset that appreciates in value over time. When a business is managed from a spreadsheet instead of through its people and systems, however, layoffs are a logical action to take to improve financial performance. The business world has even created new terms in an attempt to make it easier to fire people. By referring to people as headcount or a layoff as an RIF (reduction in force), we can depersonalize the layoff process and use it with less guilt whenever costs need to be reduced.

The real issue comes down to a simple question of whether or not the organization's leaders believe they have control over their situation. If they don't, they will give up trying and resort to short-term actions to make the bottom line look better with the hope the situation improves in the future.

As a move in response to lower profits, layoffs actually tend to make the situation worse. There are costs to the organization when people leave that can more than offset the savings in salary (see Table 5.1). It is a lack of consideration to these extra costs that keep the organization in a death spiral. As profits drop and people are laid off, the problems listed in the exhibit result in a number of associated problems that culminate into problems for customers, which leads to a further decline in sales and, hence, profits. The further drop in profits often leads to the need to cut costs again and additional people are laid off.

The problems caused by laying off workers is perhaps most obvious in the service industry, where a high percentage of the workforce work directly with customers. In healthcare, it's the doctors, nurses, receptionists, therapists, counselors, and others who face the customers on a continual basis. In hotels, revenue is generated through direct contact with the front desk agents, housekeepers, meeting and special event coordinators, concierges, and so on. In manufacturing companies, most people are usually focused on producing the products and are often isolated from direct contact with the customer. Decisions and actions that negatively affect the morale of the workers are, therefore, much less likely to be directly noticed by the customers of manufacturing companies than of non-manufacturing companies.

Table 5.1   The true cost of layoffs.

Easy to Measure

- Severance
- Unemployment taxes

Difficult to Measure

- Morale drops
- Teamwork falls apart
- Trained and experienced employees are lost (especially when business returns)
- Fear is increased among remaining employees
- Creativity and innovation is crushed among remaining employees
- Focus becomes survival instead of serving customers
- Dedication of employees to the company is lost
- Loss of "critical" employees who find other jobs

64 *Chapter Five*

There are a number of U. S. companies that continue this impotent leadership cycle for years until they eventually close their doors or are acquired by another company (others, however, remain in the cycle eventually sealing their fate).

It Hurts at First, but You'll Get Used to It

One of the sad realities in the world of business is the fact that layoffs get easier with practice. I have known executives who were visibly upset when they made the decision to layoff workers for the first time. This is a normal reaction to affecting the lives of people and disrupting the organization's culture. They go forward with the painful process, however, because they feel it's best for the company. Instead of looking at the decision as a symptom of poor leadership and attempting to understand why the organization got into its situation, however, many go about their business thinking they made the right decision and the immediate problems are solved.

The next time profits drop, the same things happens, but this time, laying off the workers becomes a little easier. It even becomes justified as ridding the organization of *poor* performers. Eventually, workforce reductions become the first thought when financial trouble arises.

In his book, *The Toyota Production System: Beyond Large-Scale Production*, Taiichi Ohno wrote, "Hiring people when business is good and production is high just to lay them off, or recruiting early retirees when recession hits are bad practices. Managers should use them with care. On the other hand, eliminating wasteful and meaningless jobs enhances the value for the workers."[2] This philosophy has been followed at Toyota for decades and continues to serve the company well today.

There may be times during the lives of some businesses that a layoff becomes necessary. When this happens, however, the leaders need to study why they let the organization get to the point where they need to reduce the workforce. Letting a worker go without attempting to understand the root cause of the need to do so is poor leadership.

Leading an organization is a very important responsibility. As a leader, your job is to lead the people in the company toward achievement of the organization's purpose, thereby satisfying the needs of all stakeholders, *including* the employees. Eliminating the people you are expected to lead is a failure in your responsibilities. If you don't make an effort to learn how you let things get out of hand, you are continuing to fail in your duties to the remaining employees.

Help the Shareholders by Putting Employees First

When a company gets into financial trouble, there are many steps it can take before reducing the workforce. Although nobody likes cutting dividends to shareholders, reducing the workforce before reducing payouts to shareholders ends up hurting the employees, the customers, *and* the shareholders. Fortunately, there are many other steps that can be taken before dividends or employees are cut.

Responsible management should work for long-term returns for investors. Cutting workers in order to pay dividends eliminates the people who have the knowledge and ability to improve the processes and systems within the company that can lead to long-term performance improvement and higher dividends for the shareholders. Reducing the workforce is often followed by nothing more than the *hope* that things will get better in the future.

As mentioned earlier in this chapter, there may be times when unforeseen external events may necessitate a decision to reduce the workforce (although the reader should remember that Southwest Airlines did not lay off a single employee, as the other major airlines did, following the September 11 attacks). The important point is that workforce reductions should be the last step, not the first, in response to a financial crisis.

The company's leaders need to have a clear plan for how the organization will address an economic downturn before the downturn occurs. The first step, which should happen well in advance of a crisis, is to build cash reserves to prevent the need for quick (and often irrational) decisions to be made when the downturn occurs. Too often, companies get into trouble because they lack the cash to continue operating during a drop in sales or an unforeseen increase in costs.

Once a downturn occurs, depending on the organization's circumstances, specific steps should be implemented to prevent the situation from becoming critical while improvements are being implemented. These steps may include the items listed in Table 5.2.

1. Delay nonessential capital spending. If money is tight, any capital spending that is not essential for the company in the immediate future should be delayed until the situation turns around. Although you do not

Table 5.2 Steps before workforce reductions.

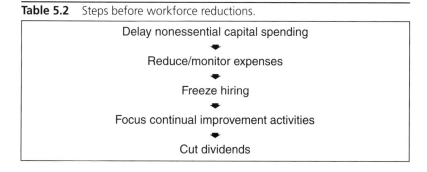

66 *Chapter Five*

want to jeopardize the future or derail the pursuit of your purpose by doing this, holding on to your cash while you determine how long the downturn will last and how to improve the situation may be necessary.

2. Reduce/monitor expenses. The second action to pursue is to closely monitor operating expenses. As with delaying capital spending, you want to assure you protect your cash during the downturn. This does not mean moving into a paperclip counting mode and micromanaging daily spending. It means clearly communicating to everyone the importance of delaying or eliminating nonessential purchases, or reducing essential purchases and giving people the means to monitor expenses in their own areas.

> A company with \$250 million in revenue implemented an expense monitoring process to reduce spending. Although the president continually preached the importance of taking care of the customer, he wanted to reduce expenses and implemented a policy of personally approving all travel requisitions. The result was a drastic drop in travel *and* sales, because people, for a variety of reasons, didn't want to bother with getting his approval before visiting customers. This is not really the type of reduction you want to see when monitoring expenses. The lack of trust the president of this company showed in the ability of his people to make sound decisions regarding when to travel was obvious, which also resulted in lowering the morale of the management team.

3. Freeze hiring. Headcount reductions may occur through attrition and delayed hiring for expansion. There is much less damage to morale when you freeze replacements for people who leave the company than when you lay off workers. When people have trust that management will not lay them off when trouble occurs, they will feel much more committed to finding resolutions to the problems the company is facing. When they're threatened with losing their jobs, or when they don't trust the leaders, however, they will feel that their efforts will not help themselves, and therefore will not work toward improvement of the processes and systems within the company.

This is one of the reasons for failure of performance improvement efforts in many companies. Whether the company is implementing a continual improvement process, Six Sigma, lean manufacturing, or any other type of improvement effort, the people must believe that the improvements will not result in a reduction of workers. Too often, however, management uses system improvements as justification for eliminating jobs, which ends up dooming the initiative to failure. There aren't too many people who will put serious effort into something that will result in more money for executives or shareholders and a loss of a job for themselves.

Successfully adopting a continual improvement philosophy also requires a leader to, as Gene Perkins, a (retired) Group Vice President at Emerson Electric, says, "get the religion." Attempts to get the people in the organization to buy into and actively practice the concept without a profound belief in, and a passion for continual improvement by management, will fail. The difference between companies that succeed with improvement efforts and those that don't coincides with their view of the operation. If they approach each production run, operation, or customer interaction as an opportunity to improve, they will tend to get better. If they approach each as solely a means to meet shipping, sales, or financial targets, improvement efforts will fail.

4. Focused continual improvement activities. Focused continual improvement means targeting process improvements at those areas most affected by the downturn. Although all continual improvement efforts should be focused on the organization's strategies, this is more direct in that it works to improve processes to support the reduction in expenses and hiring freezes.

5. Cut dividends. If things continue to worsen despite taking the aforementioned steps, cutting dividends to shareholders should be considered. Even though this action could lead to a drop in stock price, it will be short-term if the company is able to improve the situation and restore dividend payouts. Eliminating workers will delay improvements much longer than cutting dividends because the knowledge, talent, and motivation to improve the system will no longer be with the company.

A mid-sized U.S. publicly traded company was experiencing severe financial troubles. One of the actions taken by the management team to deal with the crisis was a salary and wage reduction for all employees, as well as a freezing of pay at all levels. While this action was in effect, information submitted with a proxy to shareholders (which included many employees) showed that some company officers received significant salary increases and bonuses. The devastating effect this had on the morale of the workforce was immeasurable. Also, the trust the employees had in the management team had been violated to the point that it would take many years to repair (if it could, in fact, be repaired at all).

The absolute last course of action to be taken (and it should be avoided if at all possible) is workforce reductions. As mentioned earlier, layoffs are a failure of the leaders. A truly sad situation arises when management lays off workers during the year and collects bonuses at the end of the year. Unfortunately, the system for bonuses that is commonplace in many organizations is

68 *Chapter Five*

based on results only, with no regard for how the results were obtained. This, in effect, gives incentive for management to fire workers in order to protect their bonuses, without consideration for the performance in future years. Sadly, it is fairly common for management teams to lay off workers in response to a downturn in business, while leaving their bonus accruals intact.

Although people generally don't like sacrifice, they will make them to help the organization if they feel that everyone is sharing equally in the pain. Unfortunately, this isn't always the case.

The actions listed in Table 5.2 are basically the same steps that families take when facing financial troubles. When families are in trouble, they commonly hold back on large purchases (capital), cut down on spending (expenses), and find ways to improve the situation. I have yet to hear about a family laying off the kids when times get tough. Instead, they work together to improve the situation and make sacrifices to survive. If the leaders of organizations approached the business world in the same manner, they would enable the organization to improve its situation much more quickly.

EVALUATING PERFORMANCE

Of all the practices of Western business management, one of the most destructive to an organization is the performance evaluation.

An Example

Many years ago, I worked for a company that used an elaborate system for evaluating worker performance. The system was closely tied to bonuses and pay increases for employees and used a four-point scale to rate each person (1 = high performer; 2 = performer; 3 = average performer; and 4 = poor performer).

As much as I disliked the system, until I could change the philosophy of management and the culture at the company, I had to follow it, so I rated all of the people on my team as 1 because, given the constraints of the system in which they worked, I felt they all did excellent work.

When I submitted the reviews to my supervisor for his signature, he became angry and returned them to me saying that the company never gives 1s to anyone unless they do something spectacular during the year (and, even then, the company would give no more than two or three 1s at a time). He also said that I should be able to back up any

Undervalued Employees   **69**

2s I gave with specific details about the person's performance, including why they deserved an above average rating (unless he had the same opinion, in which case, I wouldn't have to submit as much detail). 3s were considered average (and required no detail or backup information), and 4 meant the person needed to make changes or be fired.

The next rule of the system he told me was that if I gave out any 2s, I would have to balance them with an equal number of 4s (which meant that I couldn't have any above average people unless I also had people that needed to be fired).

The vice president of human resources sent out a memo to all managers explaining that a rating of 3 was perfectly acceptable and that it was important to convince employees that receiving a 3 was not a problem.

Executives liked the system because they thought it motivated people to work hard and perform. In reality, though, the system did not accomplish either objective. From the manager's perspective, a system that requires that he or she fully document the reasons for assigning any rating other than a 3 is motivation for managers to rate everyone as a 3. It is easier, quicker, and results in a lot less work for the manager. From the perspective of the employee, no matter how much managers attempt to convince them that a 3 is acceptable, it is demotivating to receive a 3 when 4 is the bottom. Most people feel that they belong at the upper end of a review, rather than the bottom.

After revising my evaluations (giving everyone a 3), I resubmitted them to my boss. He reviewed the evaluations from all of his managers and directors to make sure the grades were fairly evenly distributed, and submitted them to the vice president of human resources, who reviewed all evaluations to assure an even distribution across the company (he actually created a complex spreadsheet that statistically analyzed the ratings to assure that the results followed a normal distribution).

When they were finally returned to me (several weeks later), I had to sit down with each person on my team, explain why they were assigned a 3 out of 4, and get them to sign the evaluation. The result was demoralization of the employees and lower productivity until the feeling passed, which would take anywhere from one to four weeks. Sometimes a person would be so angry that he or she would refuse to sign the review, which would only serve as branding the person as a troublemaker.

The amount of time and money spent for a system that did nothing but de-motivate people was unbelievable. My thought at the time

70   *Chapter Five*

was that because demotivation was always the result, there had to be cheaper and faster ways for the company to do it.

Another Example

I worked with another company that used colors instead of numbers to rate people (as if this would make the process or its effects any different). In this system, the color green meant that the person was a star and ready for promotion. Yellow signified an average performer, and red meant the person needed improvement. Although the colors assigned were still very subjective in this system, at least this company held managers and supervisors accountable for the level of each employee. If a person was red during one year, it was expected that they would either be yellow, or not be working at the company at the following year's evaluation. If the person received a second red rating, the supervisor would be held accountable.

The result of this system was that the information provided was virtually useless. Managers tended to rate everyone yellow or green so it did not reflect badly on themselves . . . *Again*, a huge waste of time with very little value in return. The only advantage of this system over the previously described system was that the color ratings were not communicated to the employees, so at least the negative effect on motivation was minimal.

Focus on the System

As a very outspoken critic of performance evaluation systems, W. Edwards Deming theorized that 85% or more of the problems in organizations are caused by the system, rather than the people working in the system. This is a theory that most business people today generally accept (there are, in fact, many people who believe that the system actually causes up to 95% of an organization's problems). If we forget all about the demoralization caused by performance evaluations, one still has to wonder why we spend so much time and money on something that contributes to only 5%-15% of a company's troubles.

Are Performance Appraisals Really That Bad?

In the more than 20 years I have spent in working in the business world, I have had the opportunity to work with a number of organizations in a variety of industries. In that time, I have *never* seen a performance evaluation system that resulted in improved performance. They all come down to nothing more than a grading system that promotes patriarchy in the relationship between boss and subordinate, and serve as a regular reminder to people that their job is to please the boss instead of the customer. The evaluations that are done within these systems are subjective and often based more on whether the boss *likes* the worker, instead of the worker's true contribution to the organization (which is impossible to objectively assess).

Leaders who utilize performance evaluation systems believe in the concept that the boss knows all and is able to stop being human long enough to evaluate an employee from a completely objective viewpoint. The damage that this type of thinking has caused is profound and far-reaching. It has crushed innovation and ambition, and has contributed to the economic decline in the United States and other countries that have had the misfortune of emulating this practice.

Many executives argue this point, stating that they have never been crushed by a performance evaluation and that it is usually the poor workers who dislike the evaluation process. What many of these executives don't realize, however, is that they (and their careers) are not representative of the typical worker. A very small percentage of the workforce makes it to executive-level positions. Executives are usually very driven and successful people who have experienced very few failures in their careers. They can't assume everyone else is like them and would react to situations in the same way that they would. Besides, many executives have probably had mentors who helped them through their careers using honest but positive feedback

There have been several studies on the effects of performance appraisals. These studies usually conclude that positive evaluations do not result in a positive effect on performance, while negative evaluations do have a negative effect on performance. This is because positive evaluations are what most people expect to receive. Other studies have shown no correlation between people judged by top management as *top performers*, compared to those judged by peers as top performers[3]. Which group is a better judge of performance is anybody's guess.

Some organizations rely on performance evaluations to rid the organization of poor workers. If a worker cannot (or does not want to) contribute to the organization, perhaps the person shouldn't have been hired in the first place, which identifies a need to improve the company's hiring practices. Another explanation may be that something or someone in the organization has crushed the person's motivation and enthusiasm, both of which may have been strong on his first day of employment. It is unfortunate that many managers don't realize the deflating effect their behavior has on the motivation of their workers. In any event, whenever there is a performance issue,

72 *Chapter Five*

the manager should not wait for the performance evaluation to document the situation or take action.

What About Legal Issues?

When debates about the value of performance evaluations occur, the discussion virtually always leads to the legal issues. Many people tend to share the belief that without performance appraisals, the company is setting itself up for lawsuits when people are dismissed for poor performance.

First of all, you need to consider whether or not it's worth the cost of demoralizing the workforce just to protect yourself from a lawsuit that may never occur. Unfortunately, the large size of judgments in legal battles over discrimination and wrongful dismissal leads many to feel that it is worth the cost. Consider, though, the results of a survey of labor attorneys reported by Tom Coens and Mary Jenkins[4] where 7 out of 10 labor attorneys did not find performance appraisals beneficial in defending companies for wrongful discharge suits. The problem stems from the fact that most managers rate people average (whether or not they truly feel the person is average) and don't take the time to fully document problem areas on performance reviews.

When dealing with an employee who has performance issues, it is vital to document the situation. It makes no sense, however, to wait until the annual or semi-annual performance review to record the problem. Even when you document the issue, however, it is still your responsibility to exhaust all efforts to work with the person to improve the situation.

If dealing with problem employees is a common occurrence, perhaps you need to look at your hiring process or analyze the environment to determine what is responsible for the problems. In most situations, the problems are not poor employees but rather poor leadership.

If They're So Bad, Why Do We Still Use Them?

It is not easy for people to let go of something that they have used for many years. Performance appraisals have been used for so long that they have become a generally accepted business practice. Because of this, it is difficult for people to let go, even if they don't truly believe in their value.

I recently discussed the problems with performance evaluations with the CEO of a mid-sized U. S. company. Although he agreed that the evaluations wasted time and admitted that he had never seen a review system that actually resulted in improvement, he was afraid to stop the practice within the company until he had something ready to replace it. It is sad for the people in the company, but by leaving the system intact, the CEO feels he is erring on the side of caution. In this case, caution means following a practice that most other organizations do.

Undervalued Employees   73

Table 5.3   Intended benefits of performance appraisal systems.

- Performance improvement
- Coaching
- Feedback
- Personal/leadership development
- Bonus/pay practices
- Legal documentation for problems

If we step back and think about the intended benefits of a performance evaluation system, we can determine whether or not such systems are effective. We must lead with knowledge, and knowledge comes from learning. Regarding the performance evaluation system, learning involves clarifying what we expect from the system and monitoring it to determine whether or not the system is meeting those expectations. Table 5.3 presents the intended benefits of performance appraisals.

Each organization is different and its leaders need to conduct their own analysis to determine whether performance appraisals are achieving the intended benefits. When subjected to this type of scrutiny, however, it becomes clear that most employee appraisal systems are not effective.

Receiving Meaningful Feedback

When effectively used, the most meaningful and productive method of feedback used by many organizations today is a 360° feedback process. In the 360° process, feedback is received from the person's boss, peers, and direct reports. In the process, the feedback information goes directly to the individual requesting the feedback and nobody else. It is up to the person receiving the feedback whether or not to share the results with anyone (including his or her supervisor). This aspect makes the 360° process overcome many of the drawbacks of the traditional performance evaluation. The process enables the person to use the feedback received for development and improvement, instead of worrying about how much it is going to cost him in terms of pay, bonus, or job security.

The value of the 360° feedback is the personal development plan. The personal development plan is a document that describes the areas in which the person desires to improve (based on the results of the 360° process) and the general steps the person plans to take to facilitate the improvements. The personal plan is reviewed regularly with the individual's supervisor to assure that employee development is occurring and is effective.

Because the objective of the process is personal development, the feedback report does not receive the amount of attention that it does as part of a traditional performance evaluation does.

74 *Chapter Five*

Stop the Madness Now . . . Without Delay

Although the 360° feedback process is an excellent system for employee and leadership development, it takes time to develop and implement a system that is effective and meaningful. The first step in the process, however, is to eliminate the existing performance evaluation system. Too often, managers delay eliminating the existing system because they don't have anything with which to replace it. It doesn't matter. Traditional performance evaluation systems do so much damage to the organization that it's improvement just to stop doing it, even if there is nothing to take its place.

Organizations have improved morale very quickly by doing nothing more than eliminating the evaluation system. In addition to the improvement in morale, there is a decrease in costs because of the time required to operate and maintain most evaluation systems.

We Only Want Above-Average Workers

During leadership seminars, I often pose the question, "As a leader, what do you do with below-average workers?" I am often surprised at the number of people who answer that they fire them, improve them, or find ways to force them out of the organization.

My next question is usually, "How do you know who is below average?" The most common response is the performance evaluation system (if that seems like a perfectly logical answer, please re-read this chapter). Every once in a while, however, somebody says that they measure workers based on some objective measure (for example, time to complete a task, number of customers served, quantity of output, and so on). If we assume that these measures are objective (which in many cases, they are not), the discussion moves to the topic of basic statistics.

If the process being measured is stable, its output most likely follows a normal distribution with the average at the middle of the curve (see Figure 5.2a). If the midpoint of the curve is average, the shaded portion represents the below average results (which is equal to 50% of the workforce). If we fire or improve the performance of the below average workers, by definition the distribution would change, resulting in a shifting of the curve, or reducing the spread (or width) of the curve. This is good for the organization, but by definition, 50% of the workforce will still be below average (Figure 5.2b). In fact, no matter what we do, we will always have 50% of the workers performing below average. We can keep firing workers until there are two workers left and still have 50% of the workforce below average (even if we get down to one worker, he or she will perform below average 50% of the time).

This is a very simple concept that many people miss when talking in terms of average. Several years ago, a major metropolitan newspaper pub-

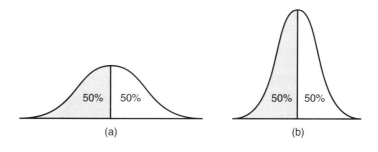

Figure 5.2 Improving below-average employees.

lished an article about a survey of history professors and their feelings on the overall performance of all U.S. presidents. The article described how disturbing it was that the survey found 50% of the presidents rated below average. One who understands basic statistics would not expect any other result.

Your job, as a leader, is to improve the system and not worry about who is above or below average. And to improve the system, you must focus attention on raising the average and reducing the spread. There are many companies that would make great strides if their leaders understood this most basic rule of statistics.

RESPECTING AND DEVELOPING EMPLOYEES

Where Do the Managers Come From?

Another indication that the management of an organization undervalues its employees is a significant percentage of the people in management positions coming from other companies. Leaders who value their employees regularly promote from within the organization. The leader who feels that nobody within the company is qualified to fill an open management position is admitting that he has failed in his responsibility to develop the capabilities of the employees or that the organization has poor hiring practices.

Leadership development is one of those areas in which it is difficult to understand why some people do not recognize its value. Most would agree, all things being equal, that someone who already knows the products, systems, people, and culture within the company is a much better choice to fill a leadership position than someone from outside the company who doesn't (see Table 5.4). It is extremely common, however, to find organizations that have management teams that predominantly consist of people who were hired in at the management level. Justifying the hiring of a manager from

76   Chapter Five

Table 5.4   Benefits of developing managers from within.

- There is a clear understanding of the person's values and working habits.
- The person understands the culture and knows the people.
- The person knows the company's processes, systems, products and/or services, policies/procedures, and customers.
- Trust is built as people see that the company is committed to their development.
- There is opportunity to see a person's strengths and weaknesses and begin development before an opportunity for promotion comes about.

the outside as a need to bring new blood into the organization is admitting that the culture is sick and needs to change.

Whatever the reasons given for the lack of a leadership development process, it usually comes down to cost. Whether it's a lack of funds to build bench strength or the inability to give a raise to someone with leadership potential to keep them from leaving the company, it once again comes from making decisions based only on measurable data with no concern about the future consequences. What many executives don't realize, however, is that the lack of a sound leadership development program results in a large cost for companies. Unfortunately, because it is one of the costs that is not measurable (see Chapter 2 for an explanation of non-measurable costs), it doesn't usually receive a lot of attention.

Grades Do Not Equal Success

Performance evaluation or grading systems in business do not tell anything about a worker's performance or ability to contribute to the organization. The same logic also applies to the grading systems in schools.

Grades in school tell a lot of things about a student, including how well the student takes tests or how much the instructor likes the student. They do not, however, predict how well the student will perform in the organization, if hired. Some of the most recently well-publicized companies that went from boom to bust in a very short period of time were well known for hiring the best people from the best business schools in the United States. The cultures at these companies also fostered a great deal of competition between people to enable the best of the best to move up into leadership positions, with no regard for the effect it had on teamwork. Unfortunately, we all know the results.

At the other extreme are companies that aren't able to hire the best due to location, industry, or size, but have done extremely well because of an emphasis on teamwork and a focus on how well job candidates fit within the company's culture, instead of IQ, grades, and internal competition. There are small companies with less than 20 employees that are more profitable and work better than Fortune 500 companies because of an emphasis on teamwork and an understanding that it is the system, not the individual, that improves performance. There have also been numerous studies that have shown that IQ is not a good predictor of occupational success.

Like many other practices used in business today, however, grade point average is used extensively as a means with which to screen candidates for hire. The hiring process is far too important to allow something as simple as grades to sway a decision.

The Mobile Manager

For years, large corporations have shifted managers among divisions to give them a broader look at the business. In recent years, the time many of these managers spend at any one division has become increasingly short. It is not uncommon for an executive to spend as little as 2-3 years (or even less) at a division before moving on to their next assignment.

This game of divisional musical chairs is a very destructive practice for the division (and, therefore, the corporation as a whole) for many reasons. One of the main reasons is that these executives never get the chance to properly learn the company or business during the short time they spend with the company. The result of this practice is that decisions are made without adequate knowledge of the potential consequences. The higher up in the organization a person is, the longer it takes them to be effective.

Another reason that divisional shifting of managers is destructive is the effect that discontinuity of leadership style has on the direction of the organization. Leadership changes result in fear throughout the organization because people don't know exactly what to expect from the new leader. Although it may not be noticeable at first, direction can shift because of differences in philosophical beliefs regarding what is important for the business. Even the smallest change in philosophy at the top can begin a domino effect that dramatically alters the company's operation over time. Companies have dramatically shifted direction after leadership changes, even when it initially appeared that the incoming and outgoing leaders were very similar. The differences were subtle, but over the course of several months or years, a lack of demonstrated interest in one or more areas can alter the course of the company. The problem is obviously magnified when leaders have drastically different management styles and philosophies.

Parent company leaders consider divisional musical chairs important to developing strong corporate leaders. Although it *can* help develop future leaders, it can also cause considerable destruction at the divisional level if the process is rushed. The process is even more damaging to the divisions

Chapter Five

when a corporate leader thinks he understands the businesses when he really doesn't.

If Not Grades, Then What?

When you decide to hire someone, consciously or not, you are making a prediction that the person is a technical and cultural fit for the company. You assume that the person has the same values as the rest of the organization and the personality to work well with the others on the team.

Grade point average, work history, and professional certifications may provide information regarding the person's level of technical knowledge, but they tell nothing about his or her ability to apply the knowledge or contribute effectively to the team.

The hiring process needs to include several rounds of interviews with several people to see if there is a perceived fit with others in the organization. There are also many methods that can help assess the personality type of the individual to determine if he or she has similar values and is a good fit for the job in question. Some companies have developed actual role-playing scenarios that put the candidate into one or more real-life situations, including actual problems to see how the person reacts under pressure and how they approach problems.

These methods require more time and money than the conventional way of hiring candidates, but are worth the effort when compared to the cost of hiring the wrong person, or more importantly, the benefits of hiring the right person.

CONTINUALLY REDUCE FEAR

One of the most devastating consequences of undervaluing employees is the fear throughout the organization. Fear can manifest itself in several ways (as shown in Table 5.5) but always results in destruction to the company. The

Table 5.5 Typical fears within an organization.

- Fear of layoffs
- Fear of retaliation for speaking up or disagreeing with a supervisor
- Fear of asking questions
- Fear of speaking up or questioning a decision
- Fear of taking chances
- Fear of making a mistake
- Fear of failing to meet objectives or goals
- Fear of misunderstanding direction

loss is huge, but like so many others, cannot be measured. One can only imagine how much more successful many organizations would be if the leaders could reduce the amount of fear that exists within their companies.

Fear within an individual can crush innovation, creativity, and motivation, and interfere with the ability to take pride in work. Written and spoken about extensively by W. Edwards Deming, fear often exists at all levels in the organization and is one of the most devastating elements a company can have.

It is the responsibility of the leaders to determine the extent of fear within the organization, identify the causes, and begin to take actions to remove it. Although it may never be possible to completely eliminate the fear, it must nevertheless be the goal.

Outsourcing

Another cause of fear and resentment today in many organizations is the practice of outsourcing jobs. Whether it involves moving existing jobs to low-cost countries or moving internal operations to suppliers, outsourcing is often perceived by existing employees as job losses.

To succeed in outsourcing and minimize damage to the organization, it is important for management to clearly understand its reasons for undertaking the project. If it is solely a cost-cutting move, it will mean job losses, increased fear, and a breakdown of teamwork and trust of remaining employees. Also, if cost cutting is the main (or only) reason, it is important to understand the total cost of moving jobs, including costs related to training, translation of instructions and procedures, travel costs, the lack of experience of the people in the new facility, as well as the costs associated with building a new facility if one is necessary.

There are unfortunately too many examples of failed attempts to outsource jobs. Problems with quality, deliveries, and damage to products during shipment have forced many companies to abandon outsourcing projects. There are also many organizations that have determined that they can cut costs and improve quality more effectively by working with existing facilities and people. Hillerich & Bradsby (H & B), makers of the Louisville Slugger, rejected the idea of outsourcing many years ago and continue to produce baseball bats (and other sporting goods including golf clubs and hockey sticks) in its facilities in the United States and Canada. The company's efforts to improve its processes and systems have enabled it to reject the idea of moving its production overseas (except in the cases where local production is a requirement of doing business).

In the 1980s, H & B was suffering from strong competition and increased costs. CEO Jack Hillerich III decided at the time to enlist the support of employees rather than implement outsourcing and short-term cost cutting to save the company. By keeping the people who could help save the company rather than laying them off (and removing the barriers that prevented them from contributing), the situation began to improve and the company regained its position as a leader in sporting goods (including owning 70% of the professional baseball bat market).

Outsourcing Is Not Always a Bad Idea

There are valid reasons for moving jobs overseas. If the company is growing and needs to be close to its customers to succeed, it makes perfect sense to locate its facilities near the markets it serves. In some markets, tariffs or laws force companies to produce products locally.

The key is outsourcing in a way that provides value to the organization is to commit to existing employees that they will not lose their jobs as a result of opening new facilities, and actually enlist their support in the project. When pursued in this manner, outsourcing can produce big gains for the company.

Innovation and Creativity

A critical element to success today is creativity and innovation among team members. Processes related to new product and service development, problem solving, continual improvement, and cost-cutting projects all benefit from the creativity of those involved. When fear is prevalent within the culture, however, innovation and creativity is stifled. Whether resulting from stress created by the fear of losing one's job, distrust, or apathy, when creativity is blocked, the chances for the organization to move beyond a state of mediocrity are very small.

IDENTIFYING UNDERVALUED EMPLOYEES

If you work for a company employing a performance evaluation system that uses grading, ranking, or some other method to evaluate people, your organization undervalues its employees. As presented throughout this chapter, these systems use numbers to make managers feel like they are being objective when they are actually doing nothing more than a subjective analysis.

Think back on the performance evaluations you have received in the past. If you received high marks, were you any more motivated to contribute, or were the results just what you expected? If you've ever received a negative review, did it motivate you to work harder, or did it just serve to de-motivate you or make you look for another job?

The process would be great if it actually worked; but it doesn't. Any company that actively uses the process doesn't understand psychology or how to motivate people to improve.

If your company uses a 360° process to provide feedback, does it allow the person being reviewed to keep the results private (even from the human resources department)? If not, there is a lack of trust by management in the employees and the organization will never perform to its full potential. Also, is the focus of the process the feedback itself or some type of development plan that is based on the feedback?

Privacy is usually the point that causes the most debate with the 360° process. Most of the process makes sense to most people, even those who tend to cling to the traditional performance review process. Questions always arise, however, with the privacy issue, regarding how to document poor performance or whether a positive 360° review can be used against the company if an employee is fired for performance-related issues. Those managers who raise these questions don't trust the employees and don't understand the role of a leader. If you have employees who you feel are poor performers but receive a positive 360° review, perhaps the problem is with you, not the employee, or maybe the review doesn't cover the important areas (in which case, it needs to be revised).

Another indicator of undervalued employees is the promote or fire policy that some executives use. The objective of promote or fire is to build the team by ridding the organization of those employees who aren't promotable.

Organizations that have followed this approach have found that they have actually depleted their talent because some who are good at what they do don't necessarily want to be promoted. If this is the case, they can either leave the company or be promoted beyond their capabilities. Promote or fire is one of those practices that makes little sense from a practical standpoint, no matter how good it sounds in theory.

Other ways to know if management undervalues the employees are fairly easy to see. If the executive staff is comprised of people who were hired into the organization at the management level, instead of people who were developed within the company, there is most likely a problem. A weak or non-existent education and training process for employees is another clue regarding management's opinion of the value of the employees. A quick review of a company's policies can also give a good indication of the level of trust the management team has in the employees. The more detailed and lengthy the policies are, the less trust that exists. Managers who attempt to describe and control all potential areas of a policy that people can violate are openly communicating their distrust of the people.

As an example, one organization wrote such detailed policies for employees that it published a 13-page policy for expense reimbursement complete with examples and strict guidelines on what would be an accept-

82 Chapter Five

able reimbursable expense. The result was that most of the people (including many managers) did not even read the policy and continued to operate as they always had, most likely violating one or more parts of the policy as it was written.

If an organization spends ample time hiring trustworthy people, policies can be brief and very general. People will follow the policies and the organization will reap the additional benefits associated with an open and trusting environment.

The rate of employee turnover is another indicator of the level of value management places on employees. When management undervalues employees, employees are not happy. When employees are not happy, they usually find other jobs.

If you're interviewing for a job at an organization, ask about the performance review. If the company has an evaluation system, ask for details. Just having one should make you proceed with caution, but you need to know if they are talking about a 360° review process rather than a traditional performance evaluation system.

You should also inquire about their process for developing leaders and why they don't have anyone inside the organization to fill the position for which you are being interviewed. Ask the same questions to several different people to make sure the responses are consistent. Remember that you're talking to a representative of the company, who, in addition to determining if you're a good fit, is trying to convince you of the benefits of the organization. It is natural for a person in this position to answer questions in the way they *want* the situation to be, rather than how it really is.

When determining whether or not to invest money in a company, it is much more difficult to discover if employees are undervalued, due to a lack of knowledge about the company's culture. Your best bet is to talk with employees about the culture at the company and ask questions about performance reviews, employee development, and so on. This is fairly easy when the company provides a consumer product or service. When the company provides a service (for example, an airline, or retail store), it's easy to strike up a conversation with an employee or watch the operation in action.

If you usually receive poor quality goods or services from a company, it can be a strong sign that the people are unhappy, which implies that they are undervalued.

Unless you're able to talk with people inside of the organization, it is very difficult to identify the warning signs in companies that do not serve consumer markets. As with other warning signs, one of the clues is the frequency of layoffs at the company, which is usually available through the media. Companies that have layoffs on a regular basis do not value their employees.

Another clue can sometimes be found in the company's website or annual report. Look at the executive profiles to see where the high level managers came from. Did they rise up through the company, or has their tenure with the organization been relatively short? Also, is the staff heavily weighted toward financial expertise or is it concentrated on the company's operation? It is these types of things, not words from management, which provide a picture of the company's values.

The inability to learn about what the company truly values is one of the problems with the type of information provided to potential investors. You can find a variety of financial information (which, as we have been taught by many companies over the last few years, doesn't necessarily tell the whole story), but there is usually no information available about how the company really operates or how satisfied the employees are. *Fortune* magazine's annual list of the best companies to work for may provide additional information about the level of satisfaction of its employees.

SUMMARY

An organization is not a tangible entity. It is a word people developed to describe a group of people working together to achieve a common purpose. As a leader, if you do not respect and value the contributions of the people that comprise the organization, your chances for long-term success are severely hampered.

Retail executives who do not value the salespeople in the stores, manufacturing executives who do not respect shop floor workers, and bank executives who feel that tellers can be easily replaced are examples that are all too common in today's business world. Unfortunately, poor financial performance is also all too common in today's business world.

NOTES

[1] Joiner, Brian L. 1994. Fourth Generation Management: The New Business Consciousness. New York: McGraw-Hill.

[2] Ohno, Taiichi. 1978. *The Toyota Production System: Beyond Large-Scale Production.* Portland, OR: Productivity Press, p.20.

[3] Crow, Robert. 2002. *70-20-10: A Prescription for Disaster.* Milwaukee: The Human Development and Leadership Division of the American Society for Quality.

[4] Coens, Tom, and Mary Jenkins. 2001. *Say Goodbye to the Performance Review: Why Dr. Deming Was Right All Along.* Milwaukee: Human Development and Leadership Division of the American Society for Quality.

6

Dirt, Clutter, and Damage

The production plant provides . . . the most direct, current, and stimulating information about management.
—Taiichi Ohno[1]

> **Definition**
>
> *The workplace is dirty and/or unorganized. Buildings, property, and equipment are not properly maintained.*

While the previous warning signs were related to the human side of the organization, the "dirt, clutter and damage" warning sign involves the physical side. Assessing the condition of the organization's workplace is actually a very easy way to determine whether the company is in decline. A company that is experiencing commercial success but has a workplace that is dirty, cluttered, or contains damaged equipment has begun its decline, even though the numbers may not yet reflect it.

Damaged equipment and dirty, unorganized work areas are a sure sign that the leaders of the company do not respect their processes and work areas or do not understand the link between their assets, the quality of the products and services delivered to their customers, and long-term performance. When analyzed from a business perspective, it becomes clear that the reason assets are purchased is to produce income for the organization.

DAMAGE AND BREAKDOWNS

A company's physical assets enable the production of income. A more profound explanation is that the assets help the organization achieve its purpose

86   Chapter Six

by fulfilling the needs of its customers. Whichever definition you choose, assets are important.

It is very common for managers to take a great deal of time to painstakingly study the costs and calculate paybacks to justify the purchase of a new asset. Unfortunately, many of these same managers fail to provide resources to adequately maintain the assets once put into service. As a result, the assets fall into disrepair, fail to contribute what they could to the company's income, and live a much shorter life than designed. New equipment should never be purchased to replace worn or damaged equipment without a clear understanding of why the equipment wore out and what will be done to prevent the new equipment from suffering a similar fate.

Leaders of healthy and focused organizations also understand that there is a direct relationship between the amount of preventive maintenance performed on assets and the level of customer satisfaction for the organization.

> I worked with a manufacturing organization that, among its many processes, performed injection molding. The company's injection presses were in a terrible state of disrepair and the tooling was visibly worn and damaged. The president of the company was very frustrated at the company's poor delivery performance, high reject rate, and high machine-repair expenses. These problems were caused by a variety of things, including the lack of preventive maintenance on the machines, tools, and equipment in the shop.
>
> I met with this company's management staff in the main conference room, which was beautiful and exceptionally clean. As I walked around the offices and the shop, however, I saw the exact opposite. There were copies of a memo from the president posted throughout the facility outlining policies pertaining to care of the newly remodeled *conference room*. Nobody was to eat in the room, hands were to be kept off the walls, and no *shop people* were allowed in the room.
>
> Through the memo, it was easy to see how little the president respected the shop people, which was most likely one of the main causes of the company's problems. It was also clear that the president's passion for cleanliness and care was for some reason strictly limited to the conference room.
>
> Ignoring the fact that he had little respect for the people in the shop (which, admittedly is difficult to ignore), the president's passion led to a conference room that was always clean and in good working order. He obviously did not have the same level of passion for the equipment in the shop, which was another major contributor to the company's problems. This attitude spread throughout the company and was reflected as a company value that maintaining shop equip-

ment was not important. This belief led to cutbacks in maintenance personnel and expenses during the company's slow periods. (Remember that the organization's values are communicated in the actions of management, rather than their words.)

After a change in the company's leadership, values began to change and the people began to see the importance of machine and equipment maintenance.

The company implemented several actions that resulted in improving the condition of its assets. Preventive maintenance schedules were developed and posted for each machine, along with instructions for performing the maintenance. The operators were trained how to maintain the machines they operated, including keeping the records updated. Although the more difficult operations continued to be performed by maintenance technicians, the operators performed many of the daily, weekly, and monthly maintenance operations.

Management at the company agreed to a one- to two-day window to allow flexibility in the monthly maintenance work, but the schedule was strictly adhered to, without exception. When managers walked through the shop, they stopped at machines and looked at the maintenance schedules to see that they were maintained and to see what type of problems were noted. When breakdowns occurred, the maintenance schedule and process for that machine were questioned in order to improve the system and prevent further breakdowns.

This occurred because the new management staff was passionate about taking care of the machines and equipment. The operators understood the need to maintain the equipment, but under the prior leadership team did not have the power or ability to do so.

Within a few months, the company began to experience improvements in productivity, costs, and delivery performance. There were still other problems with the company that needed to be addressed to continue the improvement, but they were headed in the right direction.

The conference room continued to be a place of beauty, even though it was now open to everyone.

Initiating Preventive Maintenance

Virtually every manager believes, to some degree, that preventive maintenance is important. It is amazing, however, that such a limited number of companies actually perform preventive maintenance operations.

When companies are very busy, they claim that they don't have the time to spend maintaining equipment. The people are simply too overloaded with income-producing work to stop and spend time unrelated to fulfilling orders.

88 *Chapter Six*

When times are slow, managers are pressured to reduce the workforce, which leaves nobody available to perform the preventive maintenance duties. In these instances, preventive maintenance is considered a *non-value-added activity* because it doesn't directly produce income. When managers are forced to cut costs because of a drop in sales, they tend to forget all about the organization's purpose, and cut costs that they can't see as producing income today. Cost cutting should force managers to get back to basics and focus on those things that are directly aligned with the organization's purpose. Operating the equipment that serves customers is one of the most basic processes that an organization has and failing to maintain that equipment is not in the best interests of the organization, its customers, or its shareholders.

In both situations, managers usually fool themselves into thinking they will implement preventive maintenance when circumstances change (for example, when things finally slow down or when business picks up and we can hire more people).

If you truly believe in the importance of preventive maintenance, the best time to implement it is *now*. There are no excuses or justification for not doing it.

Preventive maintenance does not apply only to manufacturing organizations. Non-manufacturing companies often rely extensively on equipment to perform services and generate income. Assuring equipment is maintained, accurate, and reliable is just as important for service organizations as it is for manufacturing companies.

In a hospital, for example, equipment breakdowns can be extremely expensive because of rental charges for replacement equipment, overtime expenses to setup and calibrate rental equipment and repair broken equipment, and the charges related to delays and overloading remaining equipment.

In a hotel, equipment breakdown can result in an annoyance to guests, a direct loss of business (guests checking out because of equipment problems), or reimbursement to guests for part or all of their stays. These costs (which are not always measurable if it leads to a loss in customers) are in addition to the direct expenses associated with emergency repair of the equipment.

The attitude toward preventive maintenance of assets by many managers is really not too surprising considering the attitude many people have toward preventive maintenance of themselves. Most people say they understand the importance of preventive maintenance of their own bodies, but fail to take action until they physically break down and are forced to visit a doctor or hospital for repairs. And if we ignore preventive maintenance of ourselves, obviously we do not believe in the concept and any chance of implementing it in the workplace will be severely hampered.

Implementing a preventive maintenance process is not difficult. There are actually several ways to initiate the process, but most involve a schedule with a description of what needs to be done and when. One of the problems many companies face when implementing preventive maintenance systems is they overly complicate the process and consequently it fails before it ever really gets going.

Refer to the manufacturer's literature to find out what the recommended maintenance steps are, and start with an operation that is small and easy to do. The process can be improved over time, but no improvements can be made without taking the first step.

Develop a schedule that identifies one to three maintenance operations in a calendar format (see Figure 6.1 for an example). Leave enough space on the calendar for the operator to record that the operation was completed on a particular day. On the back of the schedule, put a diagram of the equipment with a brief instruction for the operator to follow (see Figure 6.2). The instruction should be as visual as possible (for example, drawings or photographs) to make it easy for the operator to understand, on sight, how to perform the task. Make sure that the operator has been properly trained to perform the operation, and that the necessary tools and materials are always readily available.

The importance of following the schedule and maintaining the equipment must be continually emphasized to operators, supervisors, and anyone else related to the process. *Never* ask an operator to skip the maintenance on a particular day for any reason. Especially in organizations where the level of trust is low, people watch management very closely to determine how serious and committed they are to a new directive or initiative. They want to make sure the direction is not a passing fad before they make the emotional investment themselves. This is, unfortunately, a defense mechanism that

July 2003													
1		2	2,3	3	1,2,3	4	2,3	5	1,2,3	6	2,3	7	1,2,3
8		9	2,3	10	1,2,3	11	2,3	12	1,2,3	13	2,3	14	1,2,3
15		16	2,3	17	1,2,3	18	2,3	19	1,2,3	20	2,3	21	1,2,3
22		23	2,3	24	1,2,3	25	2,3	26	1,2,3	27	2,3	28	1,2,3
29		30	2,3	31	1,2,3								

Figure 6.1 Example of a preventive maintenance schedule.

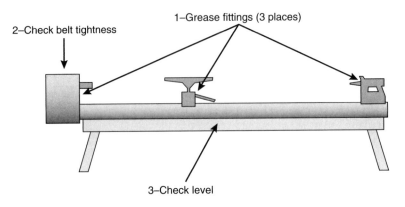

Figure 6.2 Example of preventive maintenance instruction sheet (on back of maintenance schedule).

people have developed to enable them to minimize the frustration and stress associated with today's business climate.

Preventive maintenance is a process that will continually evolve. When it appears that the initial process is working effectively, add more operations, as needed, to improve the reliability of the machines and equipment. Continually improve the process based on feedback about machine performance and breakdowns. Changes in maintenance intervals and schedules should be considered as part of the corrective action process when dealing with equipment breakdowns and quality issues. There will obviously be some operations that will require specialized training and skills to perform. These operations can be done by maintenance technicians or equipment service technicians using a slightly different scheduling format. Just remember to keep the process simple.

DIRT AND CLUTTER

One of the philosophical changes that have taken place in manufacturing in recent years deals with the view of dirt and clutter in the factory. People are slowly beginning to realize that a manufacturing operation does not need to be dirty. There are still some people, however, who cling to the notion that manufacturing is naturally dirty, and that attempts to clean it up and keep it clean are futile and not worth the investment of time.

Fortunately, there are numerous examples today that demonstrate how clean factories can become, even with traditionally very dirty processes. Japanese foundries with freshly painted equipment, well-lit work areas, and live plants situated throughout the factory floor have become common training aids in process improvement classes. The confidence that a clean operation gives customers, sometimes unconsciously, provides value to the organization. Although it usually can't be directly measured, few would argue that improved confidence by customers will benefit the organization.

One company I worked with went through a transformation in the area of dirt and clutter throughout their operation. Months of hard work and consistent behavior by plant management led to a change in culture at the company and an unbelievable change in the appearance of the factory. Weekly tours by managers and supervisors led to a consistent view of cleanliness and organization. Visitors to the plant were asked to complete a workplace appearance survey where they gave their opinions on the appearance of the plant, including suggestions for improvement.

On two occasions, customers who toured the plant for the purposes of assessing the facility for the company to become the sole supplier for their products awarded the contracts before leaving the premises. Both of these customers had visited competitors prior to visiting this company and one of the customers stated that, in reality, he had no intention of awarding the business to this company, but conducted the assessment more as a courtesy to the company's sales manager. Upon seeing the condition of the factory, however, he changed his mind and decided to award the business to the company. These two instances provided directly measurable benefits to a clean operation. But the company gained much more that could not be measured by cleaning up.

Clean work areas demonstrate management's respect for the company's processes and products. As the company in the aforementioned example discovered (and its competitors may have also discovered), the condition of the factory and work areas are immediate clues to visitors about the quality of products the company produces and indirectly the level of respect it has for its customers.

The importance of continual removal of dirt and clutter applies to service companies as well as production facilities. Dirty and unorganized work areas interfere with the performance of work and demonstrate a lack of passion and respect for the work being performed. Visit a retail establishment that is dirty and cluttered and you will most likely find unhappy employees,

92 Chapter Six

missing inventory, or a management that cares more about taking your money than serving your needs.

More Benefits of Organization

Table 6.1 presents some of the benefits associated with a well-organized and clean work environment. Some of these benefits are measurable and easy to see, while others are not easy to measure but just as important to the organization.

Table 6.1 Benefits of clean/organized work area.

- Improved safety
- Higher productivity
- Fewer lost tools and equipment
- Better inventory control
- Improved customer perception
- Earlier detection of machine/equipment problems
- Improved quality
- Improved morale

Improved Safety. Better organization in a work area decreases the chances that things will be left in aisles or walkways, which reduces the likelihood that someone will trip over equipment, inventory, trash, or furniture and get hurt. I have seen numerous factories where a lack of organization forces workers to make their way around and over pallets of inventory, which creates a safety hazard for people who are tired or not very mobile.

Another safety benefit of cleaning the workplace is the removal of oil, sawdust, powder, and metal chips from factory floors, which reduces the chance of people slipping and getting hurt. It takes time, however, to teach people that factory floors are swept with brooms and not compressed air. Although using an air hose to clean a floor is much easier than using a broom, it only results in blowing the dust and dirt to another area of the plant (and increases the likelihood of eye and respiratory injuries).

Higher Productivity. The more organized a work area is, the more time people can spend performing actual value-added work instead of wasting time searching for tools and equipment or walking to other areas for items that are used frequently. When the workers are involved in the process, they will assure that the area is organized in a way that makes their jobs easier.

Fewer Lost Tools and Equipment. A commonly used method for organizing work areas involves painting outlines to identify where a tool or

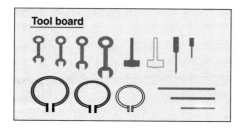
A tool board (left) is a board where tools hang. An outline of each tool is made to identify where each tool is located, and to see when a tool is missing. In this example, a hammer and clamp are missing.

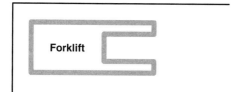
Painted lines on the floor can show exactly where moveable equipment is stored. At left is an example of lines painted on the floor in a corner of the plant to show exactly where a forklift is to be stored when not in use.

Figure 6.3 Using outlines to identify locations.

piece of equipment is stored (see Figure 6.3). This allows people to visually recognize if equipment is missing and gives them clear instructions as to where the equipment is to be placed when not in use. It should be clearly understood by everyone in the process that all equipment will either be in use or in its identified storage location. In cluttered and unorganized operations, missing equipment may not be noticed for several days (if at all). Cleanliness and organization, however, enables missing equipment to be noticed very quickly.

Better Inventory Control. When inventory is well organized, it becomes much easier to know how much is on hand at any given time. Even when a computerized inventory control system is used, visual methods are effective because more people become aware of current levels. Also, while computer systems are not always accurate, visual methods are. Figure 6.4 presents an example for deploying an organized visual inventory control system for an injection molding plant.

Improved Customer Perception. If customers are exposed to the workplace (as with many service industries), customers will judge the organization by the cleanliness and organization of the facilities. For example, an automobile repair facility with a high level of technical competence may not be judged as such if it has a dirty, cluttered, and unorganized shop area.

Earlier Detection of Machine/Equipment Problems. It is much more difficult to see cracks and leaks in equipment when the equipment is

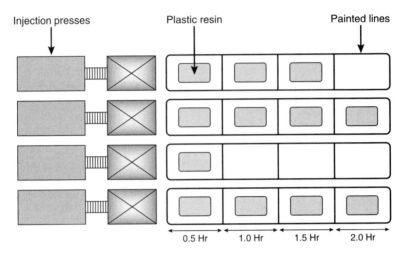

In the injection molding operation above, boxes were painted on the floor, which held 30 minutes of inventory (plastic resin) to be used in the press. The operator (and visitors to the operation) could always see exactly how much raw material was on the floor waiting to be used, and the operation never had more than two hours of raw material on the floor at any given time.

Figure 6.4 Example of visual inventory control.

dirty than when it is clean. Keeping machinery clean allows these types of problems to be noticed and repaired before they become critical. Another old time view of manufacturing is that oil-lubricated machines always leak. This is simply not the case. Leaking oil causes dirt to build up and hide problems, and provide a less appealing work area.

Improved Quality. Machines operate better when they are clean. When gauges and controls are dirty and uncalibrated, machine capability is affected and quality suffers. Even when parts are still produced within specification, there is most likely increased variation in the part's characteristics, which can cause increased assembly time, quicker wear, or increased problems in use.

Cleaning and Organizing with 5S

There are many ways to improve the cleanliness of a work area. The most commonly used method, developed many years ago in Japan, is referred to as 5S (also referred to as 4S or 6S, depending on how the steps are organized). The process involves five steps (each starting with the letter *S*) that can transform a messy work area into a clean and highly organized area. It is important to note that the 5S process works as well in office and service areas as it does in the factory.

In addition to improvements in the cleanliness and organization of the work areas, the 5S process has another benefit. It teaches the people in the area to work as a team. 5S gives the team an identity and clear boundaries with which to work. The process teaches teamwork at a very basic level by giving the group control over the organization of the areas where they work. In fact, if the people in an area cannot effectively work together in the 5S process, there is no chance that they will be able to handle more sophisticated process improvement activities.

Before beginning any type of cleanup effort, it is important to take pictures of the area. These pictures will become the *before* photos of the area and will be used to demonstrate to visitors to the area, as well as those working in the area, how far the people have come in the process. After the initial gains have been made, the pictures will also be useful to keep people motivated to continue the process. It is perfectly natural to forget how things were in the past, and become discouraged due to a perceived lack of progress. Pictures, however, will objectively remind people how things were before the process began, and can help to keep enthusiasm and energy at a high level.

The 5S Process for Cleaning/Organizing a Work Area

The steps in the 5S process include Sort, Scrub, Set up, Standardize, and Sustain.

Sort: The first step in the cleanup process is to sort the items in the area. This includes tools, equipment, procedures, file cabinets, and so on. Color-coded tags are very helpful in this step, and speed up the process.

Those items that are used on a continual basis should be tagged green. Items that are used in the area, but less frequently, are identified with yellow tags, and items that are rarely or never used should be labeled with red tags. To keep the process from getting bogged down due to disagreements about which color to tag an item, place white tags on anything that requires further discussion. At the end of the process, the team returns to the white-tagged items to discuss the group to which they belong.

Scrub: The second step in the 5S process is to clean, and repaint if necessary, the equipment in the area. In addition to machines and related equipment, this also includes desks, walls, carpeting, and anything else in the work area. Also, any necessary repairs to the

96 Chapter Six

equipment are done at this stage. Leaks are repaired, gauges are repaired or replaced, holes are patched, and any other type of problem is repaired.

Set Up: Once the area is completely cleaned, the items that were tagged during the SORT stage are set up in a logical fashion. This involves bringing all of the green-tagged items back into the area and arranging them in a way to allow the people to access them easily.

The yellow items are moved outside of the immediate work area to allow them to be accessible when needed, but not interfere with the items used frequently.

The red-tagged items are moved completely out of the work area or discarded. Because they are rarely used, it will not affect productivity to any measurable degree if the worker needs to leave the area to get them. This is a difficult step for many people because of the natural tendency to not want to discard something *just in case* it is needed.

Standardize: Standardizing the process involves making cleaning and organizing a normal part of the process. This means setting aside time each day to give people the opportunity to clean the work area and put tools and equipment in their respective areas. This has to become a normal part of the process, and must be followed without exception if it is going to work.

Sustain: Another difficult aspect of the 5S process is to sustain the gains made in the previous four steps, and to continually improve the cleanliness and organization of the area. Too often, teams that go through the process and make great strides in their areas stop there, and over time let things slip back as they were. It is important not to let this happen.

Companies that have been successful with the 5S process have made the cleaning equipment the same status as equipment used to operate the process. Brooms, mops, and other cleaning tools are labeled and stored in the area within easy reach of the workers. I have even seen workers paint their brooms with the company colors to assure the brooms fit neatly within their work areas.

Whenever the process stops (breakdown, no work, before and after breaks, and so on), workers sweep and clean the area, to prevent it from getting dirty again. Standardizing the cleaning operation is one of the most difficult parts of the 5S process because it involves a change in mindset of the managers and workers in the area. Initially, management will need to constantly remind the workers of the importance of cleaning. If you want to do something quickly and easily that will send a clear message about the importance of cleaning, walk through the shop and stop and clean up something that needs to be cleaned. The story will spread and the message will be clear. Also, never walk by trash on the floor, no matter how small, without picking it up and discarding it.

Gene Perkins, a group vice president (retired) at Emerson Electric Company, picked up a broom and swept the floor in a plant of one of the company's divisions that he felt needed to improve the cleanliness of its factory. Although it took him less than five minutes to sweep the area and pick up the dirt, the story of his action was told for several months afterward and began the change in the culture at the company.

IDENTIFYING DIRT, CLUTTER, AND DAMAGE

Of all the warning signs of organizational decline, this is probably the easiest to identify. A quick look at the work area can tell a lot about the company and where it's headed.

If you're interviewing for a job with a company, ask for a tour of the facility so you can see first-hand how much management respects its assets. If your host won't give you a tour, at least insist on one before accepting a job offer. Companies that utilize proprietary processes will be less likely to let visitors into the plant, but in my experience, no matter what they think, very few actually have processes that are truly unique.

Companies that are exceptionally clean and well organized are usually very proud of their facilities and are very open about opening their plant up to visitors (this, of course excludes facilities where safety is a concern, or ultra-clean processes are deployed).

> Several years ago, a successful regional grocery store chain was purchased by a national chain. A few years after the purchase, the condition of the back of the stores began to deteriorate. An increase in garbage and dirt was evident, and broken shopping carts and rusting refrigeration equipment were stored sloppily outside the back of the store. Not long after that, the company announced a significant loss since the purchase of the chain. This was not a surprise, given the condition of the stores. The signs of decline were fairly clear.

Even if you can't manage to get a tour of the facility during your interviews, notice the condition of the offices, buildings, and landscaping. If offices are cluttered, buildings are deteriorating, or landscaping is ignored, exercise caution before accepting a job offer from the company.

If you're considering investing money in a company, it is more difficult to determine the condition of the facilities. If the company operates retail outlets, notice how clean and organized they are. Look around the outside of the building, as well, to determine if the condition of the exterior is similar to the interior.

If the company in which you are considering an investment doesn't operate retail stores, identifying this warning sign is more difficult. If they have local facilities of any type, it is worthwhile asking for a tour. If you can't get one, at least assess the conditions outside of the facility. If the landscaping and building exteriors are not well maintained, consider investing your money elsewhere.

SUMMARY

As with many of the concepts presented in this book, many of the benefits of a clean, well-maintained work area are not easily measured, but are significant. Although it is much easier to see in a service operation because of direct interaction with the customer, the benefits are just as great for manufacturing operations.

A manager of an operation who says he or she is interested in continual improvement or Six Sigma but runs a dirty and cluttered workplace is only giving lip service to the improvement initiative. Improvement requires respect for the operation, the people working in the operation, and the customer, and a dirty and unorganized work area shows a lack of respect for all three. Without a fundamental change in beliefs about the level of cleanliness and order to a workplace, sustained improvements will not be possible.

Companies invest a lot of capital in their assets and it is vital to make sure that the assets contribute to, rather than interfere with, the organization's success.

NOTES

[1] Ohno, Taiichi. 1978. *The Toyota Production System: Beyond Large Scale Production.* Portland, OR: Productivity Press.

7

Operational Fragmentation

*If you try to take a cat apart to see how it works, the first
thing you have in your hands is a non-working cat.*
—Douglas Adams[1]

> **Definition**
>
> *The level of teamwork is low and the company is operated as a
> fragmented group of departments and people instead of as a single system working together to accomplish a common purpose.*

Which is more important: How well an individual department performs or how well the organization performs? When I ask this question, without hesitation I always get the same response: The organization. The answer is obvious. If it is so obvious, however, why do we focus so heavily on departmental and individual performance, often to the detriment of the organization as a whole? Although it would be great if managing a company was as easy as setting goals and measures for individual departments and tying bonuses to the achievement of the goals, we are reminded daily that this approach does not work.

DEPARTMENTAL GOALS

Although we may have been taught in the past that the *atomistic* method of management is an effective way to lead (that is, breaking the organization into smaller components in order to understand and manage it), history proves otherwise. Organizations are far too complex to focus on the pieces while assuming that the whole is holding together. Overemphasis on

100 *Chapter Seven*

departmental goals and measures leads to fragmentation that is counterproductive and interferes with organizational success.

It is unfortunately a common practice to set departmental goals that are emphasized and met repeatedly by managers who don't seem to understand (or care about) the damage caused to the organization, its customers, or its stockholders. The following section presents examples of goals commonly used by companies that can, and usually do, lead to decline.

Common Departmental Goals and the Damage They Cause

The following are some commonly used departmental goals that might appear to be helpful to the organization, but usually end up hurting performance and contributing to organizational decline.

Procurement: Reduce/Contain Material Costs. A goal of reducing or containing material costs, while ignoring the total cost of materials to the organization, will usually lead to poor quality, late deliveries of incoming materials, or both. Purchasing professionals will meet the goal, especially if it's in some way tied to pay or bonuses, with little regard to the customers of the materials (including manufacturing, production planning, and the external customer). Another probable effect of meeting the goal is increased tension and a loss of teamwork between purchasing and manufacturing, because lower quality materials interfere with the manufacturing team's ability to meet its goals. Purchasing professionals cannot really be blamed for this outcome because, within the current system of most businesses, they are doing what they feel is necessary to keep their jobs or maintain their bonuses.

Engineering/Product Development: Product Development Project Completion Dates. Although it's always beneficial for a product development group to meet its dates for product release, it is destructive when the dates are met by cutting corners, ignoring customer requirements, or releasing incomplete information to those who need it to produce the product or service. Too often, products are released with errors or quality is poor due to mistakes resulting from incomplete or incorrect documentation. When this happens, manufacturing and warranty costs increase, customer satisfaction drops, and future sales are hurt, even though the project goal was met and may even have been accompanied by a short-term rise in sales.

Manufacturing: Meeting Monthly Shipping Goals. This goal is one of the most widely misused goals for manufacturing organizations. In order to meet monthly or quarterly financial goals, plant managers are measured and rewarded on the basis of meeting monthly shipping targets.

The goal is often met (at least on paper), because of increases in overtime, shipping of defective or substandard products, and possibly even keeping the books open into the following month until the numbers are met. The goal is artificially met and everyone feels good, except the customer and those inside the organization who realize the problems that this practice is creating. Tying shipping goals to bonuses is also a sure way to turn plant managers into dictators.

Sales: Meeting Sales Forecasts. It is very common to hold salespeople accountable for meeting sales forecasts. The irony in this practice is that often it is the sales managers or executives who set the forecasts after rejecting the initial forecasts submitted by the salespeople who are the closest to the customer. Holding salespeople accountable for meeting sales forecasts, either through bonuses, commissions, or pressure, will often result in the person meeting the forecast. Unfortunately, the way in which the forecast is met is not usually in the best interests of the company. Pressuring distributors to buy more than they need, offering incentives that reduce the company's margins, selling customers more than they really need, and promising deliveries that cannot be met are all ways in which salespeople strive to meet the forecasts. Teamwork also breaks down when salespeople start blaming other areas for their inability to sell (for example, quality problems from manufacturing, design problems from engineering, and so on).

There are numerous examples of non-manufacturing organizations that have sold customers services that they really didn't need in order to meet forecasts or goals set by management. Lawsuits and lost customer credibility have resulted for auto repair, home improvement, and financial services organizations that have followed this practice.

An example to illustrate how far people have gone in misunderstanding and misusing goals was seen during a recent visit to a popular department store chain. As I walked through the ladies cosmetics department, I overheard a manager discussing performance with a salesperson. The manager told the salesperson that she was doing well with eyeliner because she had exceeded her goal for the month, but she was far behind in sales of lipstick and needed to put more effort in selling lipstick over the next week. The manager did not seem to care whether or not customers wanted lipstick. It didn't matter whether or not the store stocked the correct amount and types of lipstick, the manufacturer offered the quality and colors that women wanted, or if the store charged too much for the lipstick. The focus was on meeting a goal and the message to the salesperson was to sell lipstick, not serve the customer.

Keep Expenses Within Budget. One organization I worked with used departmental budget variances in the calculation of bonuses. If a department's expenses for the quarter were in excess of the budget for the

102 *Chapter Seven*

same period, the manager would not receive a bonus for that quarter. As can be expected, managers usually stayed within their budgets, but did so by holding expenditures at the end of each quarter, even if those expenditures were necessary to service true customer needs. Training and travel to customers and satellite plants became non-essential in the eyes of the managers because these things affected their bonuses.

There is nothing inherently wrong with monitoring budgets and requiring explanations for instances where expenses exceed the budget in a given period. It is important to keep in mind, however, that budgets result from guesses made at some point in the past. It is not an exact science as nobody can foresee everything that will happen throughout the year. As the year progresses, expenses will exceed budget during some periods and will fall below budget in others. The desire is to have the differences net out in the end.

Tying bonuses to expenses in each period leads managers to tamper with the operation in an effort to prevent expenses from exceeding budget in any one period. Tampering in order to make the numbers work virtually always leads to damage to the organization or its customers.

Facility Opening Dates. Although it is important for new facilities to open as quickly as possible to enable the organization to begin recouping costs and producing income, using bonuses or threats can lead to opening a facility that is not yet completed, resulting in long-term damage for the facility and the organization. For example, it is common for hotels to open without all of the services available because of equipment that is not ready for use, which can lead to a loss of customers (whereas not opening may lead to loss of a stay, there is less chance of losing a customer).

The key to using goals is to understand that they are only guesses or hopes for the future. They are what, under the correct circumstances, leaders believe will drive the organization toward sustained success. Most executives understand what sales levels, shipment levels, or product mix is required for the company to be successful (or at least think they do). What is needed, however, is for these goals to be met with real numbers and through system improvements, instead of artificial measures or by hurting the overall performance of the company. Whenever goals are used, however, they should not be tied to pay and they should be used to learn where the system broke down or to identify where improvements need to be made.

Using system feedback in this manner requires an understanding of the Plan-Do-Study-Act (PDSA) cycle originally presented by Walter Shewhart. The cycle is a way for people to learn about a process or system by developing, testing, and validating theories for improvement. Because goal setting involves a desire to improve a process or system, it can be approached in the same manner as process improvements, using the same method and tools. The

In an effort to reduce inventory shrinkage (that is, the amount of inventory lost due to a variety of reasons including spoilage, damage, inventory inaccuracy, and so on), the southwest region of a national chain of fast food restaurants implemented a goal for store managers. The regional director implemented a quarterly bonus for store managers when shrinkage was below 3% of total inventory value.

The goal was met fairly quickly and the southwest regional director was praised by corporate executives for his success in addressing the problem. The director was asked to make a presentation about his initiative at a national meeting and other regions were directed to implement similar goals.

Over the following several months, the restaurants within the southwest region began to experience a steady drop in revenues. Market research studies also began to show a corresponding drop in customer satisfaction. The biggest contributors to the customer dissatisfaction were low scores on: Availability of Desired Food Choice and Overall Quality/Freshness of Food. Upon further investigation, it was discovered that store managers were reducing purchases of slower-moving inventory and using food beyond freshness dates, both of which were strategies used by managers to reduce inventory shrinkage.

PDSA cycle is presented here as a method for goal setting/system improvement. Organizations comfortable with using the Six Sigma approach to process improvement could just as easily use the DMAIC (Define-Measure-Analyze-Improve-Control) approach in the same manner as PDSA is presented here.

For example, if a proposed change is intended to reduce cycle times in the manufacturing process, thereby increasing on-time delivery of products to customers, the proposal is a theory that needs to be tested to further learn about the manufacturing system (PLAN). The proposal should be tested on a pilot basis to assure that it does, in fact, improve cycle times and result in improved delivery performance (DO). By studying the results of the test, those involved in the process gain knowledge about how to improve the process (STUDY). If cycle time was improved, the change should be implemented (through process changes, job restructuring, training, revision of procedures, and so on). If there was no improvement, the change should be abandoned, revised, or re-tested (ACT). Either way, knowledge is gained, which is important for all involved in the process. Refer to Figure 7.1 for an overview of the PDSA cycle.

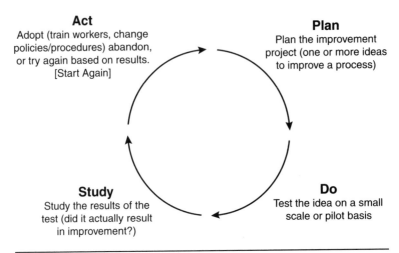

Figure 7.1 Overview of the PDSA process.

Organizational fragmentation through goal-setting is very common and can show up in several ways. However it appears, it always results in organizational decline. The key is to understand that it is happening and to make the necessary changes that will transform the organization into a single-minded system.

PDSA and Goal Setting

One of the problems in getting people away from the current mode of goal setting is that most managers don't know of an alternative way to move an organization forward. Even if the situations listed earlier in this chapter blatantly exist within an organization, goals and numeric targets have been the mode of operation for so long that most people know of no other way to attempt to make improvements or meet business challenges. According to W. Edwards Deming, "It's all right to have a numerical goal, but only the method will get you there; it's only the method that counts. Anything else will mean loss. All you have to do is walk around and see it."[2] PDSA enables focus on the method.

The PDSA cycle is a proven way for an organization to learn and improve. It has been applied to the process for setting objectives in some highly successful companies for many years. When consistently applied for several years, the process can lead to significant overall improvements in key areas.

Another advantage of the PDSA process is that it realistically addresses the improvement process. When initiating an improvement project, it is not realistic to think that a person can develop a plan that can effectively assess all possible aspects of the project. Especially at first, plans are guesses based on experience and knowledge about similar initiatives. Even the best plans usually require adjustment as the project moves forward. Objectives can be missed due to a variety of reasons including plans that are poorly developed or not implemented well, or due to incorrect assumptions about cause and effect. This is to be expected and should not be considered as a failure as long as learning takes place.

The PDSA cycle automatically enables adjustment to assure that the plan remains aligned with the objective. The cycle also keeps everyone focused on the method of improvement, rather than the goal. Although in practice the two are often confused, it is the method and not the goal that results in the improvement.

The process starts with an identified need to improve in a specific area of the company. The need can be an obvious problem for the organization or be identified through the company's strategic planning process. The result is the identification of key initiatives or projects that address areas in need of improvement.

Plan. Once the initiative is defined, including a clear objective and scope, the leader of the project works with the executive (or the manager) ultimately responsible for its success. Together, they identify a measure (there may be more than one) that will provide feedback to the team regarding whether or not the desired improvement is occurring. Because the objective is improvement, rather than finding out who to blame or hold accountable, the measure is a feedback mechanism to help the team (and company as a whole) determine if improvements are being made. The measure is not tied to team member bonuses or pay increases. The measure also helps provide the team with a clear definition of the desired improvement.

The measure may already exist. If not, the team will need to work to implement the measure quickly to establish a baseline with which to gauge improvement.

Using problem-solving tools (for example, Cause and Effect diagram, Pareto Analysis, brainstorming, and so on), the team identifies steps to be taken to improve the process or system as defined in the initiative. Once the team determines which steps to take to improve, it will develop a plan for implementing the change(s) on a small scale for testing.

Do. Implementing the steps developed by the team requires a clear plan to assure that the results can be analyzed clearly to determine whether or not the desired improvement is occurring.

106 *Chapter Seven*

Study. As improvements are implemented, the team (as well as the sponsor or management team) uses the measure to determine if the steps identified are being implemented effectively and if actual improvement is occurring.

As the initiative is reviewed with the executive team or sponsor, the steps taken as well as the future plans are discussed. If improvement is not occurring, the management team works with the project leader to determine what can be done to make the project team more successful. Although the project team is working on the initiative directly, the management team is ultimately responsible for its success, and this process enables management to actively participate in the improvement.

Act. This phase involves continuing with the steps identified or changing course and working on other alternatives determined during the PLAN phase. If the team's actions appear to have been successful, ACT may include expanding the change(s) to other facilities or areas of the company, changing policies or procedures, training employees, or other actions that will assure the improvement is standardized within the company. It could also involve letting the team continue with the project on the path they currently are. If the team is not being successful, this step could involve providing additional resources to the team to help them stay on schedule with the plan.

The PDSA cycle repeats itself as the team pursues other areas that may have been identified during the first PLAN phase but were not considered as vital as the initial actions the team chose to take.

The following section provides an example of the PDSA cycle in goal setting. The process, when implemented correctly, results in moving the focus by management from the *goal* to the *method*. Focusing on the method is the key to keeping people from feeling they need to meet goals at any cost and allows them to center their attention on improvement.

PDSA and Goal Setting—An Example

During the strategic planning process, it was determined that the company needed to make improvements in the safety of its manufacturing facilities within North America.

Plan

The Vice President of Human Resources and Vice President of Manufacturing identified the Director of Manufacturing as the team leader for this initiative and worked with him to determine the appropriate measure for the project. The group determined that the number of lost-time accidents was the best measure to gauge whether or not safety is improving. The data for the measure already existed and it had been recorded for the past few years, but was not used for any improvement activities.

The safety improvement team initially analyzed the data from the last 12 months in a control chart to determine whether the system was stable and, if so, what its current capability was (see Figure 7.2).

After charting the data, it was determined that the system was stable and that any improvements needed to come from a change in the system. Using standard problem-solving methods, the team analyzed the data to look for common elements in the classifications of accidents and to determine if there was any significant difference in the results from any of the individual North American factories (see Figure 7.3).

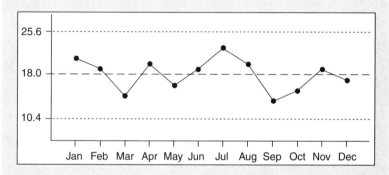

Figure 7.2 Lost-time accidents for North American plants.

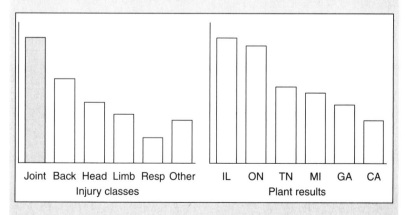

Figure 7.3 Analysis of lost-time injury data.

From the data, the team constructed a cause-and-effect diagram to determine the most likely causes of joint injuries (the most common type of injury as listed in Figure 7.3). Although the plant result data in Figure 7.3 is not particularly meaningful due to the size and type of work performed at the factories, it will be used by the team to select a location for testing improvement actions.

The team selected repetitive motion as the most likely cause of joint injuries, and brainstormed ways to reduce the number of joint injuries by focusing on repetitive motion. As a result of their analysis, including dialogue with supervisors, manufacturing engineers, and health consultants, the team decided to implement a job-rotation program where assemblers would rotate among jobs to reduce the number of motions they perform in any given month.

Do

The process was implemented within the Ontario, Canada plant and involved a great deal of training to enable workers to rotate to another job without adversely affecting the quality of work performed. The joint-related injury measure was closely monitored in the Ontario factory during this test period, along with quality measures to assure that the plan did not result in improvement in one area while hurting another.

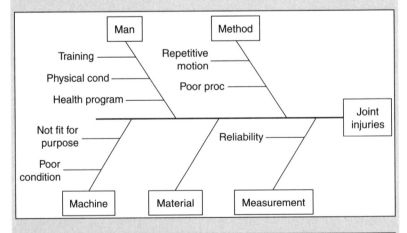

Figure 7.4 Partial cause and effect analysis of joint injuries.

Study

The results of the test demonstrated that the rotation plan resulted in a reduction of injuries. During the test period, quality declined slightly, which resulted in plans to adjust the training process for workers prior to rotating jobs.

The team met with the Vice President of Human Resources and Vice President of Manufacturing several times during this phase to keep them up-to-date on the progress of the team.

Act

After several iterations of adjusting the training process and time period between job rotations, there was a significant reduction in job-related joint injuries, which resulted in a reduction in overall injuries. The team also noted that quality improved along with the employee satisfaction level among the workers involved in the process. As a result, the rotation process was expanded to the other North American plants.

As part of the job rotation trials, the team discovered that training and work instructions needed improvement (both areas were identified on the original cause-and-effect diagram from the PLAN stage).

As the process was rolling out to the other factories, the team returned to its cause-and-effect diagram to select the next cause to address, which involved improving the way in which the physical condition of job candidates was assessed. Overall, the team completed several iterations of the PDSA cycle to address the injury issues within its North American plants and reduced the incidence of lost-time injuries by 80% over a three-year period.

Management's involvement in the process was to provide direction and understand the methods deployed by the team to improve the situation. The objective was to improve workplace safety and their focus was on the method to achieve the goal. The team felt completely supported by management and therefore could focus on continual improvement of the situation rather than only meeting a target.

WHAT'S BLOCKING TEAMWORK?

CEOs often cite lack of teamwork as a major problem for their organizations. "If people would only learn to work together, the company's performance would improve." It's a frustrating problem for corporate leaders because they see many of the problems that a lack of teamwork causes for the company.

110 Chapter Seven

What they don't often see, however, is that it is often their own policies and actions that prevent people from working as a team.

If the organization is managed as a fragmented group of departments, plants, or teams, that is exactly how the people will act. People will spend their time and energy working to optimize their component with little regard to the effect it has on the other components or the organization as a whole. No matter how much people may want to work together, there will be barriers that prevent them doing so. The resistance caused by the system will be too strong to overcome. Whether intentional or not, people will learn to do what they feel is necessary to survive even if it means taking actions that are not in the best interests of the customer.

If you hold the purchasing department accountable for reducing procurement costs, operations accountable for meeting delivery dates or reducing service times, quality assurance accountable for product quality, and salespeople accountable for sales volume, the organization will become a disconnected group of specialists who meet their own goals while ignoring the needs or contributions of other areas. In other words, extreme caution must be exercised when you set goals for individual people and departments because of the risk that they just might meet them.

The purchasing manager will bring the cost of incoming material down, but cause problems for manufacturing, quality, and the customer. Manufacturing will meet delivery dates, but only by shortcutting quality, which will increase warranty costs and inventory levels, and since customer satisfaction decreases, reduce incoming orders. Salespeople will increase sales, but by selling products that can't be produced, pressuring distributors to increase their inventories, promising unrealistic delivery dates, or selling the customer something they don't need.

Any level of teamwork can completely fall apart under these circumstances because one department can only achieve its goals by interfering with another's ability to do the same. And if you really want to kill any hope of getting people to work together, tie a person's bonus or pay increase to the achievement of a goal. The result will be entertaining to watch but hasten the destruction of the organization.

These aren't far-fetched examples. They are situations that occur every day in companies in virtually every industry, including manufacturing, healthcare, retail, food service, and others. Most organizations are far too complex to set individual goals in such a way as to assure they can only be met in a way that improves performance. And counter to the way that many people think, there is nothing that anyone in the organization does that doesn't affect one or more areas of the company. When management takes actions that penalize people for considering areas outside of their own, teamwork will break down and organizational performance will suffer.

These gaps in the system that interfere with teamwork are created by top management and grow exponentially as they move down the organization. If management doesn't recognize the gaps and take responsibility for closing them, there is little chance that anyone else will.

It Happens at All Levels

Failing to understand and focus on the system is a common problem at all levels in all types of organizations. When fragmentation occurs at the top of an organization, there is little hope for the rest of the organization to work as a unit.

An example involves a large division of a Fortune 500 company that is comprised of a group of organizations that serve similar industry segments. The division was originally created to provide customers with more of a *total solution* than any of the individual company's competitors could. Besides the marketing and selling advantages of these companies, the division was also designed to have cost and price benefits over competitors because of the size of the organization. The vision developed by the president of the division was one of sister companies pooling their talents, sharing best practices, and working together to provide value to the customer that could not be matched by anyone in the industry. Unfortunately, as a direct result of the division president's actions, it was a vision that has never materialized.

Although he talked team and total solution, the president's actions supported the concept of company versus company and fragmented support to the customer. On a regular basis, he held performance review meetings with individual company executives, and held them accountable for the sales and profit performance of their company. Because of this, people in the individual companies began to have conflicts over which company would receive credit for the sale and profit on orders that involved multiple companies. Intercompany sales, in which pricing was fixed at a much lower level than commercial orders, became a low priority for the companies. When the end of a period came around, each of the companies would focus on shipping their commercial orders first (that is, those with higher sales values and profit margins) and intercompany orders last, because of the financial impact and the need to meet their shipping and profit goals.

Because intercompany shipments were virtually always received late, shipments to commercial customers that involved intercompany products were also late because of the lower priority, resulting in poor customer satisfaction. In fact, a survey conducted by one of the new companies in the division found that customers were more satisfied with the company's service before they became part of the parent organization (the exact opposite of the vision expressed by the division president).

The continual fighting and poor service between the companies even forced some to purchase products from competitors instead of from companies within the division. Although this practice angered the division president, it was easier for the company executives to deal with his anger than the effect lower performance would have on their bonuses. The lack of consistency between the president's vision and his actions became the going joke among company managers, albeit a joke that also caused a lot of fear and stress within the organization.

If the division president in the previous example really wanted to achieve the vision of becoming a total package supplier, he should have concerned himself more with total division performance than individual company performance. Division executives should have been held accountable for total division performance, as well, including tying the bonuses of division team members to the performance of the total organization because this was how the president defined the system. If a company's profits were down because of an increase in intercompany shipments and the division's profits increased because of increased total package sales, then the companies are performing as expected and everyone (including the customer) benefits.

Even though, in the above example, the division president may have probably accepted the reasoning that an increase in intercompany shipments resulted in lower financial performance, the extreme pressure placed on company executives for profits led to a natural tendency to de-emphasize intercompany orders. His knowledge and background led him to believe that emphasizing individual component performance would naturally lead to success for the system. Unfortunately, this belief resulted in the exact opposite, which led to problems for the employees, customers, and himself.

DEFRAGMENTING A COMPLEX SYSTEM

The degree of personal transformation that is necessary to defragment the organization so people can begin thinking and acting as a system is often underestimated. When explained in a classroom environment, systems thinking appears to be a very simple concept that many managers think they already practice.

The fact is, however, that implementing a systems approach within an organization is a very difficult process that requires continual reflection and analysis of one's own actions. The journey toward a system level of leadership is a never-ending one, as it is virtually impossible to achieve a total level of systems thinking. When a leader begins to understand and truly believe in the concept, however, the results for the organization can be dramatic.

When discussions about the rise of post-WWII Japan, and specifically the Japanese automotive, steel, and consumer electronics industries transpire, one hears a variety of opinions on how they became a global economic power. Everything from quality circles, lean manufacturing, and statistical process control (SPC), to product dumping, government protectionism, and luck is offered as a key to their success. There were undoubtedly several factors that came together at the right time that led to the rise of Japan, but one of the most important was the arrival and influence of W. Edwards Deming.

In his book, *The New Economics,* W. Edwards Deming credited the philosophy of viewing the organization as a system as the "spark that ignited Japan." During his first seminar with Japanese executives in 1950, Deming presented a diagram of a production system and explained that viewing the organization in this manner could enable them to compete successfully with the rest of the world.

Obviously, quality circles, SPC, lean manufacturing, and other tools and methods played a hand in the success of many Japanese companies, but these things were the *how* more than the *what* in the process. To be successful with these tools, they must be built on a foundation of systems thinking (that is, you've got to have the *what* before attempting the *how*). They worked in Japan because the people understood that the tools were there to support the system, rather than optimize the individual components.

Systems thinking is an exceptionally difficult concept for Americans, who by nature do not think in holistic terms. The United States was founded on the premise of protecting the individual and maintaining the rights of the states (that is, the system components) rather than the whole. The American Dream, rugged individualism, and the Lone Ranger all reflect a culture of fragmentation and individualism. Because of this, success in moving the organization toward systems thinking will first require a change on a personal level. You need to be strong enough in your beliefs in a systems approach to handle the resistance that accompanies a move away from policies and practices that are traditionally a part of business. It also requires the ability to reflect about actions, beliefs, and cultural elements within the company that are interfering with optimization of the organization as a whole. It takes the strength and courage to go against what you have, possibly for many years, believed was common sense. Although the more one learns about systems thinking, the more your idea of common sense changes.

114 *Chapter Seven*

A Simple but Expensive Example of Fragmentation

A large international company owned a site that was shared by two of its facilities. The decision to locate the two plants on the same site was based on the fact that one of the facilities provided a key raw material to the other facility. Although the plants were in separate divisions, the decision was made to locate them next to each other to improve communication and reduce logistics costs. The concept was very much in line with systems thinking and, if successful, would provide definite advantages to both facilities. Unfortunately, there were some significant barriers that prevented the plan from being successful, and as a result, both facilities experienced higher costs and worsened communication.

Although both plants were part of the same parent organization, they were in separate divisions and were run as separate entities. The division presidents were held accountable for the performance of their respective divisions through performance reviews and bonus plans. The presidents, in turn, held the plant managers accountable for the profit and loss of their plants. The result of all of this accountability was a group of people who cared more about their own performance than that of the company as a whole.

The managers of the two plants on the site continually argued over the amount of raw material shipped from the supplier plant to the customer plant. Each facility installed several millions of dollars in duplicate measurement instrumentation because of a lack of trust in what the other was reporting. The situation became known throughout the industry and reflected very poorly on the company's reputation.

Although management was talking *whole*, they were managing *parts*. The result of this was increased costs, decreased communication, and a tarnished company image.

A change of this nature should never have been made without a review of the systems and beliefs that affect the performance of each facility. Only an enlightened management team with a holistic approach to business would have foreseen the potential problems with this plan and taken the steps to avoid the problems encountered.

MORE BARRIERS TO SYSTEM PERFORMANCE

There are many system level barriers within organizations that interfere with the teamwork and success. Paying commissions to sales persons is one of the practices that many people have accepted as the way those in sales are compensated, but don't understand the damage it can do to the organization and its customers.

Many use commissions as the way to motivate people to sell products. It is interesting that we think we need to use incentives for salespeople to motivate them to do their jobs, when we don't consider paying commissions to purchasing agents, manufacturing engineers, or warehouse personnel for doing their jobs. Unless you have the feeling that salespeople will waste time and not sell if they are not provided with extra motivation, the argument for sales commissions does not make a lot of sense.

When a large portion of a salesperson's compensation is based on selling products or services, that's what they will spend their time doing, even when it doesn't make sense for the organization. When helping another salesperson serve a customer, or helping people inside of the organization better understand what the customer's needs are interferes with the compensation, these things will not be a priority.

Another problem with commissions can occur when orders are taken that cannot be shipped because of incomplete information. For example, when shipping information is not available when the order is ready to ship, products can sit for long periods of time waiting for somebody to obtain the proper information. The person trying to obtain the information is not usually the salesperson because he or she is off chasing other orders. And when products sit, the company loses money.

Teamwork between salespeople can also break down because of disagreements over who gets credit for a sale and who will serve the customer after the sale.

Probably the person who suffers the most from paying commissions to salespersons is the customer. Nowhere is this more evident than in retail stores. Generally, when a retail store pays its people on commission, the first salesperson who approaches you owns you for the duration of your visit. Whether or not that person helps you, or if you need help at all, that person receives the commission from anything you purchase. In many instances, you are untouchable by other salespeople. The whole practice can be extremely annoying for the customer.

Whenever I discuss the subject of commissions in retail stores, it never fails to get people talking about bad experiences they have had with commissioned salespeople in stores. The negative effect the practice has on consumers makes one wonder why it continues to be such a widespread practice.

There are a number of possible explanations for implementing a commission-based pay system: (1) lack of trust in a person's desire to perform without the incentive; (2) the belief that the organization can't afford to pay the person unless they perform; (3) it's always been done that way, and you can't imagine doing it any other way; or (4) fear that your biggest producers will quit if you take away their incentives.

> A well-known department store chain uses commissions to compensate its salesmen in the men's suits and sport coats department. The salespeople will bend over backwards to help customers who they believe will buy on that particular visit, but are visibly rude to those who do not look like they are going to make a purchase. On my one (and only) visit to the department for a purchase, I had to wait at the register for about 10 minutes because the salesman who helped me was busy with another customer. During this time, two other salesmen were standing at the register doing nothing. They wouldn't take the time to handle my transaction because of the possibility of interfering with their ability to serve another customer who might walk into the department, and because they weren't making any money from the sale.

Lack of Trust

If you don't feel that people will perform without incentives, you need to either change your belief in people or your hiring practices. If you have hired the right people, they will want to perform well. If they don't, it is probably due to something that management has done to interfere with the person's intrinsic desire to contribute. It's up to management to determine what the destructive practice was (which may not be the same for everyone) and correct it.

If you don't feel that you've hired the type of people who are intrinsically motivated to perform well, you probably do not have an effective hiring system. The process for hiring people is one of the most critical for organizational success. It takes time to carefully screen candidates to determine whether there is a good fit for the person within the organization. Unfortunately, in most cases, this is not well understood. See Chapter 5 for more information on hiring practices.

Can't Afford People Without Commission

If you don't think you can afford a salesperson unless you pay them on the amount of sales they produce, you probably need to consider whether the practice is really producing more income for the company. As mentioned earlier, paying commission to salespeople tells them that selling is their most important (or only) responsibility. Selling at a profit or selling something that the customer really needs becomes secondary.

If the organization is too small to afford to pay salaries to salespeople, it should probably adjust its policies to pay based on organization performance rather than sales volume. It should also consider paying everyone on the same basis, rather than just the salespeople.

If you don't feel your product or service will sell without a heavy incentive for salespeople to push it on customers, it's probably time to step back and determine whether or not you have a marketable product. This is a business problem; not a sales problem.

It's Always Been Done That Way

Doing anything just because it's always been done that way is poor leadership. Some of the practices that have been carried through the generations of business management may have made sense at the time they were developed, but times change and practices need to be continually analyzed to understand whether or not they are producing intended results. Effective leadership requires continual assessment of practices to determine whether or not they contribute to, or interfere with, the organization's success.

Fear of Losing the "Biggest Producers"

Companies that have moved away from a commission-based pay system for its salespeople rarely lose anyone because of concerns over loss of income. Obviously, base pay needs to be adjusted to account for the loss of incentive, but in most cases, people would much rather work for the best interests of the customer and company, neither of which tends to occur when commissions are used to motivate salespeople.

If a compromise cannot be worked out with a particular salesperson to account for the loss of commissions, it may be better for the organization and the salesperson in the long run to let him or her go to another company. Systems thinking enables members of the team working together to achieve the organization's purpose. When one member of the team is more interested in working outside of the organization's system, they are probably causing more damage than is immediately apparent.

Layoffs Do Not Equal Systems Thinking

Another situation where systems thinking falls apart is during layoffs and budget cutbacks. When a leader decides to reduce the workforce or cut budgets, managers scramble to protect their *turf* and fight to keep as many people in their team as possible. Teamwork falls apart and the needs of the organization as a whole take a backseat to individual and department interests.

IT'S A MATTER OF LEADERSHIP

The simplest explanation of systems thinking is that the job of a leader is not to manage individual departments; the job is to lead the organization. The

118 *Chapter Seven*

individual functions only exist to help the organization meet its purpose and serve its customers, and need to be led as such. When the organization is led from a functional perspective, however, department managers will be forced to focus on their own areas and be less concerned about the effect on the overall system.

When problems occur within an organization, there is a tendency to blame the worker closest to the job where the problem was discovered. This line of reasoning carries into other areas as well, including performance appraisals. Those who tend to believe in traditional performance appraisal systems feel they can adequately assess a person's performance by reviewing the quality of his or her output. There are so many factors that affect the job a person does, however, that it is virtually impossible to adequately assess individual performance. As an example, Table 7.1 lists some of the factors that affect the quality of output for a person in a manufacturing job and a billing clerk in a healthcare facility (the list is by no means exhaustive). The same type of analysis can be performed on virtually any job in any type of organization.

HOW TO IDENTIFY OPERATIONAL FRAGMENTATION

Identifying a fragmented organization is a little more difficult than some of the other warning signs, since virtually every organization is fragmented to some degree. The existence of other warning signs is, in fact, usually a sign of operational fragmentation.

When you're working within an organization, there are clues, however, that identify a lack of systems thinking. One of the simplest ways is to look at the physical layout of the offices. Whenever people representing similar functions are situated with each other and segregated from other functions, it is usually an indicator of fragmentation. Every company I've worked with that did not operate in a holistic manner segregated its people by department or function. In some of these companies, the divisions were so blatant that negative comments about the other groups were commonplace and accepted by management. In one organization, the *iron curtain* was the nickname of the area where the engineers were located. The office area reflected an open design, with only cubicle walls separating people. Every support function was located in the open areas with the exception of engineering, which was also open, but was separated from the other functions by a wall with closed doors.

The non-engineering functions joked about the lack of support they received from the engineers and that they were protected by the iron curtain. The vice president of engineering knew of these comments, but blamed those

Operational Fragmentation 119

Table 7.1 Factors that affect worker performance.

The quality of a product produced by someone in a manufacturing position is influenced by many factors, including:

- Company hiring practices
- Availability of technical help
- Noise level in shop
- Time to do the job
- Amount of training
- Quality of training
- Process/Machine capability
- Quality philosophy of supervisor/ management
- Clarity of drawings
- Knowledge of customer requirements
- Respect of supervisor
- Calibrated instruments
- Condition of tooling
- Uniformity of material

- Workplace ergonomics
- Safety of workplace/tooling
- Availability of instructions
- Shop conditions
- Skill of worker
- Trust in management
- Dirt/clutter in shop
- Availability of suppliers

- Quality of suppliers
- Respect for supervisor
- Number of hours worked
- Quality of product design
- Ability to ask questions

The ability of a hospital billing clerk to issue a timely and accurate statement to an insurance company depends on the following:

- Company hiring practices
- Workplace ergonomics
- Availability of resources to keep up with workload
- Ability to access other areas
- Reliability of equipment
- Availability of instructions
- Time to do the job
- Amount of training
- Skill of clerk
- Quality of training
- Accuracy of services/supplies/pharmaceuticals put into system
- Trust in management
- Quality philosophy of supervisor/manager
- Knowledge of billing codes
- Respect of supervisor
- Respect for supervisor
- Number of hours worked
- Ability to ask questions

120 *Chapter Seven*

making the comments rather than looking at his own actions as the cause. Only after this man was replaced did the walls come down and the engineers begin accepting their role as one of support to the rest of the company.

When the people in the company are physically organized by process, product, or service provided, there is usually a much greater extent of teamwork. When organized in this manner, their focus becomes the output of their process, which is serving the customer, rather than their individual function.

Another way to identify the warning appears in the way the company approaches projects. As an example, in non-systems-thinking companies, product development projects are handled by the engineering or development group alone and *handed off* to the manufacturing team to figure out how to produce it. Systems thinking in design means that every area affected by the product or service is involved to some extent in the project.

Quality Function Deployment (QFD) is a commonly used tool to assure a systems approach to product development and other projects. QFD utilizes a series of matrices to keep the customer's desires in the forefront throughout the process. Each of the matrices are closely linked and address different parts of the process, including design of the product, development of the process to produce the product, and identification of the process control characteristics to assure the quality of the product. The links, which originate from the voice of the customer, keep the team focused on the whole process, rather than their own specific area of expertise. Appendix C presents an overview of the QFD process, including the steps for applying QFD to product design projects.

There are other obvious signs within the company that point to a lack of systems thinking. If the company is organized into business units that compete for the same resources and have conflicting goals, the leaders have fragmented the organization. This also applies to organizations in which every function is designated as a profit center, which charges other departments for its services. Nothing can break an organization apart more quickly than requiring every department to generate a profit.

In one organization, the profit center concept was practiced to such an extent that managers spent a good deal of time invoicing other departments for their services. Requests for help from support departments began with a quote from the support department defining how much the receiving department would have to pay for their services. A great deal of non-value-added time was spent chasing internal invoices and arguing over interdepartmental charges. Some managers began going outside for help, which often resulted in lower quality work (because of the lack of understanding the outside contractors had in the company and its systems), and higher total costs.

In theory, the profit center concept appears to make perfect sense. To some, it looks like a way to make sure that support departments add value and that the people in them strive to provide high quality service to their internal customers. In practice, however, the focus on profits (and meeting budgets) exposes problems with the concept. It forces everyone to look at their own business, rather than the business of the organization.

The lack of a concerted effort to develop suppliers also demonstrates a lack of understanding that suppliers are an important part of your system, and as such, need to be developed like any other component for the company to be successful. Significant damage is caused by not understanding that suppliers are just as important as the internal components of the system. Unfortunately, many leaders fail to understand this point. Those who do understand, however, have shown marked success in their businesses.

If you're interviewing for a position at a company, ask questions about supplier development to understand the commitment to the process and ascertain how well management understands the system. Ask how many suppliers the company has; the number should be relatively small. In particular, ask how many suppliers the company has for any particular type of product or service. When managers understand systems thinking, they make sure the company is working with one supplier for a given product.

Ask about the process the company uses to develop new products or services. You may get different answers from different people, or negative descriptions by people who aren't included in the process but should be. Both of these types of responses point to fragmentation.

If the job involves a bonus, make sure you are clear on the way the bonus is calculated. If the bonus calculation involves meeting goals that other people and departments do not have, the leaders manage with an atomistic view and you will need to decide if you want to join a fragmented company.

Another way to identify fragmentation is to ask about the company's purpose. If the organization has no clear and consistently understood purpose, no system can exist. There will only be a group of independent people and departments fighting for things that they alone feel are important.

Outsiders wishing to invest money in companies have a much more difficult time identifying this warning sign. If the company has retail outlets, visit a store and look at the level of teamwork between salespeople. Be wary of the company if it becomes clear that the sales people work on commission.

Another possible way to learn the extent to which a company is fragmented is to read newspaper and magazine articles that have been written about its problems and practices. Look for clues regarding whether or not its facilities, departments, and teams work with each other. If there is information on its bonus structure, you may be able to ascertain whether its management practices encourage fragmentation.

SUMMARY

Defragmenting an operation is one of the most difficult aspects of leadership because it tends to go against the way many leaders think. It takes a continual effort and constant reflection to identify the barriers that interfere with operating the organization as a single entity with a common purpose. Organizations that are successful with the concept realize that holistic thinking is a never-ending process that requires constant attention.

NOTES

[1] Adams, Douglas. 2003. *Salmon of Doubt: Hitchhiking the Galaxy One More Time.* New York: Random House.

[2] Glauser, Ernst C. 2000. *Does Anybody Give a Hoot About Profit? Deming Speaks to European Executives.* Zumikon, Switzerland: The Swiss Deming Institute.

8

Improving the Organization's Health

A thought which does not result in an action is nothing much, and an action which does not proceed from a thought is nothing at all.
—Georges Bernanos[1]

The preceding chapters present explanations and examples of the warning signs of an organization with a weakened immune system. If allowed to continue, the fundamental problems that cause the signs to occur will weaken the organization to the point where it will interfere with the ability to withstand external events that can send the company into a death spiral from which it is difficult to escape.

If you identified with any or all of the signs, it is time to take action to improve the health of your organization. Whether you lead a department, a division, or an entire company, you have a responsibility to your team, your customers, your stockholders, and yourself to begin addressing the problems interfering with long-term success. Even if the organization appears to be performing well, it's important not to assume success today guarantees success tomorrow. Too often, executives take credit for their organization's success when it is mostly due to a strong market for their products or services. A real test of a leader's ability, however, is when economic conditions weaken.

THE NEED FOR TRANSFORMATION

With most leaders in today's business world, transformation refers to a fundamental shift in beliefs about people, organizations, and society. When used in the context of organizations, the term *transformation* refers to challenging the assumptions about existing systems and practices to assure they are contributing to, rather than interfering with, the organization's ability to achieve sustained levels of success. It means creating a culture that is

123

124 *Chapter Eight*

addicted to improvement and openly embracing of change. This process often involves a fundamental change in the culture, systems, and operating philosophy. The extent of the transformation obviously depends on the organization's specific situation. It may require development of a new purpose and operating philosophy or reestablishment of them if management has allowed the company to drift away from its roots. Loss of purpose is a common situation when current leaders are one or more generations removed from the company's founder.

Transforming an organization is not a public relations exercise. It does not involve celebrations, posters, or well-rehearsed speeches. In fact, the more glitter and polish surrounding the message, the more people will distrust your intentions. Although people want to believe in their leaders, they have been disappointed too many times by confident (and sometimes untrustworthy) executives to buy into everything they are told. Believing in a leader's false intentions is one of the most demoralizing and depressing experiences a person can have. It is also an experience that has unfortunately been all too common in recent years.

What does need to be communicated about a transformation is information surrounding the actions taken to address the company's problems. When communicating to those in the organization, however, fight the urge to overpublicize the actions to prevent the message from losing its sincerity. Your passion and enthusiasm will become apparent through your dealings with people, and in the number and type of actions taken. An executive's visit to a work area or handling of a difficult situation will send a message much more quickly and deeply than a poster or memo.

REQUIREMENTS FOR SUCCESS

Requirements for a leader to succeed in transforming an organization include personal involvement, a commitment to the transformation, a great deal of patience, an ability to reflect on one's own beliefs and actions, and a clear plan of action.

Personal Involvement

If you are the leader of an organization, you must be personally involved in its transformation. If you aren't involved, others won't see it as important and the organization will not change.

Too often, transformation is delegated to a quality or human resources professional. Although these people may be the internal experts on the subject, their role should be one of consulting rather than leading. Transforma-

Improving the Organization's Health **125**

tion affects the entire organization and needs to be led by someone who is viewed as a leader of the entire organization.

Commitment to the Transformation

There is an inherent problem with the term commitment in today's business world. Because it has been overused by corporate executives and consultants, especially in the context of organizational transformation and quality, few people will believe in statements regarding commitment to anything except short-term initiatives. Pressure from boards of directors, as well as the typical leader selection process, has created a large number of attention-deficit business leaders who don't seem to be able to commit to anything that requires a long-term focus. It is not difficult to develop a list of companies that deliver poor product or service quality, even though the company's CEO publicly espouses a commitment to excellence.

In a speech to shareholders, the CEO of a large U.S. company discussed the plans to address the severe financial troubles the company was facing. He admitted that the company had problems and needed to make vast improvements in quality and product design to pull out of its death spiral. As the speech continued, he stated that the company's absolute top priority was to become profitable again. Many who heard this statement questioned the CEO's commitment to improvement in product quality and design. If he truly believed in the importance of quality and customer satisfaction, or understood cause and effect within the complexity of organizations, he would realize that the top priority is to make the best and highest quality products in the world. If the focus is customers, profits will come. If the focus is profits, customers will go. Also, emphasizing profitability is not going to inspire people the way that making the highest quality and most respected products will.

The CEO's words were also interpreted by the employees that layoffs were going to occur. If the organization's top priority was to make the best products in the world, the people would become engaged in the process and layoffs would not be an inevitable conclusion. Because profitability was the objective, however, layoffs were pretty much a foregone conclusion. Massive layoffs did, in fact, occur and the company unfortunately continued its death spiral.

In many cases, a lack of clear commitment does not necessarily reflect on the CEO's character. Leaders often do not understand transformation

126 *Chapter Eight*

well enough to know what they are committing to. There are not too many people who would intentionally implement an action to interfere with continual improvement, even though this is how it often appears. Getting people to actively participate in improvement activities requires much more than merely asking for their input. It requires creating an environment where people believe in the company's mission and trust the leaders.

To effectively lead the type of transformation described in this book, a leader must become a student of organizational change and truly understand what it means to him or her and the organization. The leader must be willing to learn as much about systems thinking and process improvement as he or she has about finance and accounting.

Incompatibility Between Tools and Culture

One of the most common reasons for failing to successfully shift to an improvement-focused culture is attempting to implement the tools and techniques associated with improvement within a traditional management system. The two are not compatible with each other and there will be a constant struggle that will result in damage to the organization. When this occurs, the management system will eventually win and the organization as a whole will lose.

In most cases, managers only begin working to change the organization when a crisis occurs. This is unfortunate because the best time to begin making improvements is when things are going well and the organization can afford to be patient enough to allow the changes to take hold. When the organization enters a crisis mode, the stockholders usually expect quick change and won't be patient enough to believe that a long-term transformation is the answer. Too often, however, managers are afraid to interfere with an organization that appears to be performing well. Individual plants, divisions, or entire companies, whether they are profitable or not, will exhibit one or more of the warning signs when there are problems that require action. As mentioned throughout this book, a strong economy often covers up problems in an organization. When the market for a company's products or services declines, however, those organizations with inherent problems will usually suffer greatly, often resulting in drastic cutbacks, employee layoffs, and so on.

Another factor that interferes with commitment to organizational change is the personal change that must occur before a leader is able to make an organizational commitment. One cannot simply *flip a switch* and become committed to transformation. And except in the most unusual of circumstances, it does not happen after merely attending a seminar or reading a book. It can take months or years for a person to change fundamental beliefs enough to be willing to put his or her job on the line by plotting a course that runs counter to the way most businesses are run today.

Along with commitment comes the courage required to make the change successful. If you are truly committed to transforming the organization at a profound level, you will be courageous enough to defend your actions to board members and others who will continually test your beliefs. You will be challenged for not laying off workers when revenues decline; you will be challenged for stopping the practice of paying commissions to salespeople; and you will be challenged for entering into long-term agreements with suppliers based on total costs rather than purchase price. You should think of the challenges as a test to determine if you have transformed enough on a personal level to begin working on change on an organizational level. If you aren't up to the task of defending your actions and becoming a teacher to those around you, you aren't yet able to transform your organization successfully.

Patience

Leading the process of organizational transformation is a highly complex task that requires a great deal of patience to be successful. Because you are attempting to get people to change the way they think and interact with each other, you need to be prepared to face difficulties. You will need to become a coach and work with people on a continual basis to understand a new approach to running the business. It is important to not express your passion as anger, however, to prevent creating another barrier to change resulting from the fear that will be introduced into the culture. I have seen leaders who have used fear out of desperation to get people to change. When this occurs, all that happens is that people appear to change when the leader is around but go back to their old ways at all other times. These people also tend to develop negative feelings toward the transformation because of its association with fear and humiliation.

Some people will understand and accept the transformation quickly while others may need more time to re-learn virtually everything they have been taught and experienced throughout their careers. Because of the psychological impact associated with any type of change, there will be some people who are unable or unwilling to accept the new direction. If you are clear about your expectations and have taken the time to coach and help people to understand the reasons for and the requirements of the changes, however, this group should be very small.

Fundamentally changing one's own beliefs or actions requires a person to recognize a need for personal change. This recognition can be triggered by an event, periods of reflection, or a combination of both. To make the process even more difficult, what causes one person to change will most likely not cause another to change.

Leaders often spend too much time and energy worrying about the people who will not change. It is much more important to work with those who are accepting the new philosophy and slowly expand the influence of this

128 *Chapter Eight*

group by assigning them more power and responsibility within the organization. If you verbally support those who are willing to change but continue to promote or give power to those who won't, the organization will not change. (*As crazy as this sounds, it is a fairly frequent occurrence*).

Perhaps the person with whom you will need to be the most patient is yourself. Personal transformation is a journey, not an event. Your commitment to the journey will regularly be tested and require many difficult decisions. As you stay on the journey, however, you will begin to recognize the importance of people and how the interactions between people and departments determine the success of the organization. You will also begin to see mistakes you've made in the past and how these mistakes have contributed to the organization's problems.

The most important part of the journey, however, is recognizing that it has no end. Transformation naturally leads to learning and development of people, teams, and the organization. Once you understand this, you will understand that it can never stop. Stopping the process means stopping your ability to grow. And an organization cannot stand still: if it is not growing, it is dying.

The Ability to Reflect

In the context of this book, to reflect means to examine your actions and beliefs to determine whether they support or hinder your chances for success. Although it is one of the most basic requirements for learning, it is something that many people tend to ignore. Organizations have reduced staffing levels to the point that people shudder at the thought of taking time away from their jobs to do anything. Without reflection, however, there is no learning or growth and fundamental change is not possible.

Organizational reflection consists of a group of people meeting to talk about the organization's beliefs, values, and systems to understand whether they interfere with success in achieving the purpose. It is an important way for organizations to learn, grow, and achieve sustained levels of success.

Leading an organization through the transformation process is not easy. In an effort to change the behavior of others (and possibly yourself) you will not always make decisions or take actions that are in the best interests of the new direction of the company. If you are able to reflect on your actions, however, you will learn quickly when you are the one who is interfering with the organization's ability to change. But if you don't recognize your mistakes and aren't able to learn from them, you will confuse others in the organization and greatly reduce your chances of success.

The ability to reflect, personally or organizationally, requires a clear mind, honesty, humility, and a desire to improve. It is a process that requires a good deal of practice to perfect but has huge rewards for those who are able to do it regularly. Reflection results from an application of the Plan, Do, Study, Act (PDSA) cycle to individual and organizational thoughts, behaviors, and actions. A person or team can reflect on a particular situation or use a series of questions to help guide the process.

Figure 8.1 provides one framework for reflecting on a situation that didn't go as well as you had hoped. It is based on the PDSA concept to analyze what you expected to happen, what actually happened, and why. If you can learn enough from the process to improve the outcome when a similar situation arises in the future, you are learning and improving yourself.

A similar method to analyze a situation uses a problem-solving and root cause analysis tool known as the *Five Whys*. With this method, you ask yourself or your team to describe what happened and why it happened. Ask why to your answer and continue to ask why until you come to a conclusion that you can do something about (see below for an example of the Five Whys). Using the Five Whys enables the team to get to the root causes (and there are often several causes) of the problems being analyzed.

Guided reflection uses questions to help a team focus on a central issue that needs attention. As with any form of team reflection, this process works best when the process is facilitated by a person who can keep the team talking

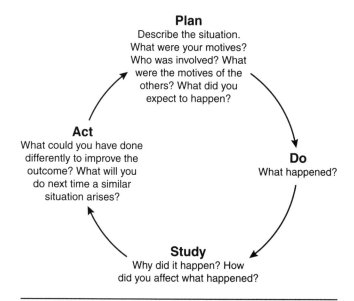

Figure 8.1 Reflection and PDSA.

130 *Chapter Eight*

enough to dig deeper and deeper to understand the current realities within the organization. A facilitator can also make sure the team keeps its focus inward rather than looking to blame its problems on someone or something outside of the organization.

Appendix D presents several questions to help a team understand the culture, systems, and barriers to transformation in an organization. Appendix A (explained in detail in the next section) provides an organizational assessment which focuses the discussion on the warning signs that may exist in the company. Although the assessment is intended more as a planning tool than a guide to deep reflection, the team should use whichever method works best for them in improving the organization. Whereas the questions in Appendix D facilitate reflection on a specific element of the business system or culture, the assessment tool in Appendix A gets the team to look at the organization at a very high level.

A Five Why Example

Following is an example of applying the Five Whys to an element of organizational transformation. A team using the Five Whys to address a cultural issue should be prepared to invest enough time to dig deeply to get to the root cause of the problem being addressed. There is no magic to the number 5 when asking why. Sometimes the root cause of the problem can be discovered before the fifth why, while other times it may take more than Five Whys to fully understand the cause. The more the team uses this method, the more valuable the process will become. The example below took the team about 45 minutes to complete.

> **PROBLEM:** The number of submitted suggestions at the Richmond injection molding plant is far below the other plants in the group.
>
> **WHY** is the number of suggestions at the plant so low?
>
> The plant manager does not emphasize the system to his management team and the others in the plant.
>
> **WHY** doesn't the plant manager emphasize the suggestion system?
>
> The plant manager does not feel that workers are able to contribute anything that would significantly improve the performance of the plant.

Improving the Organization's Health **131**

WHY does the plant manager feel this way?

Most of the plant manager's training and experience occurred under the company's previous management team which did not emphasize worker involvement. His beliefs and actions mirror the culture of the company under the previous management philosophy.

WHY does the plant manager still operate under the previous management philosophy?

He had operated under the old philosophy for many years and feels comfortable managing in this way. He also believes that, although we [*the corporate management team*] talk about the new philosophy, we still only care about the profits produced by the plant each quarter.

WHY does the plant manager not believe us [*the corporate management team*] when we talk about the importance of worker involvement?

We have not taken enough time to work with him to clarify expectations, teach him how the suggestion system fits into the new company philosophy, and help him with its implementation. Also, we need to be careful in the words we use with him to understand when he misinterprets our message. We have probably spent more time with him talking about profits and shipments and sent the wrong message by not emphasizing culture and employee involvement as the cause of improved financial performance.

ACTION: Visit the plant and begin a formal process of coaching the plant manager. Clarify expectations about employee involvement. Also, review bonus plan to see if it can be changed to prevent overemphasis on current profits and shift the plant manager's focus from short-term profitability to long-term sustainable improvement.

The team in this example came to the conclusion that they are a part of the problem because of the mixed signals they have sent to the plant manager. Although the initial thoughts were to replace the plant manager, they decided that the company owed it to him to provide coaching and clarify expectations. Within two years, the plant became the most profitable within the group and was second among employee suggestions and involvement in improvement activities.

132   *Chapter Eight*

The situation in the previous example is not limited to manufacturing facilities. Bank presidents who do not respect the intelligence or value of tellers, managers in healthcare facilities who do not respect the knowledge of nurses, and store managers who do not respect the knowledge of cashiers and salespeople are all situations that can be reflected upon and brought to the surface through the use of the Five Whys.

The method you choose to stimulate the reflection process doesn't really matter. What is important is to get a team of people to engage in meaningful dialogue with each other to understand the true causes of the problems the company is facing. If people don't think of the process of reflection as important as doing their day-to-day work (or if there aren't enough resources to allow people to take the time to reflect), the team won't learn and the organization will not grow.

A Clear Plan of Action

Fundamentally changing an organization is a major task that requires a clear plan in order to be successful. If your organization experiences several of the warning signs presented in this book, you may feel overwhelmed by the task and wonder where to begin. In addition to the results of the reflection exercises, the warning sign assessment in Appendix A will help clarify where your company's problem areas are and can be used to help you decide where you can begin improving the organization's health.

The purpose of the assessment is to aid in the process of organizational reflection. Because of this, the process is most effective when it is completed by a team rather than one individual. The value of the process is in the discussion and revelations rather than the answers. Because of this, it is important to record the thoughts and revelations that arise during the discussions, in addition to the scores. These will greatly aid the development of the plan once the assessment is completed.

Depending on the culture and level of fear within your organization, you may want to have the assessment completed by several teams comprised of people representing a variety of levels and functional areas. If there is a high level of fear within the company that may inhibit an open and honest dialogue, it may help to have a trusted person within (or outside of) the organization to facilitate the discussion and present the results anonymously to the management team.

After completing the assessment, the scoring grid will to help you to determine which areas of the organization are in the most need of attention. The scoring is meant to be used as a guideline, however, rather than an exact measurement. The management team will need to decide where help is needed most. As mentioned earlier, when dealing with a system, focusing on one component while ignoring another can cause more problems than it fixes.

The questions relating to purpose are assigned higher weights than the other signs because of the importance of purpose to the success of any organization. This is to encourage the transformation process to begin with establishment or recommitment to a purpose. In reality, if there is no purpose, there is no organization. There is only a group of individuals coming to work, putting in their hours, and going home. The purpose appeals to something deeper and enables commitment on a personal level.

Once the assessment process (including the scoring grid) is completed, you will have a list of areas identified that are in need of improvement. Depending on the size of the list, it may be worthwhile to group related items together so high-level projects or initiatives may be identified. See Affinity Diagram description on page 134 for a suggested method for organizing the list.

Don't Overload

Once you have a list of problem areas to be addressed, you will need to look for relationships and prioritize them to determine what needs to be addressed first. The priorities established are based on the information from the assessment to help you keep from taking on too much at one time. It is better to make progress on one or two of the most important projects than to attempt to work on ten projects and get nowhere.

A few points to keep in mind when prioritizing projects include: (1) look for the high-leverage projects; (2) look for areas where improvements can be made quickly; and (3) focus on projects that have a great chance of success. If any project meets all three of these criteria, your chances for success are high.

High-leverage projects are those that will have a positive effect on more areas of the organization than the other projects. These are the projects that will improve more than one area of the assessment. Because they are often (but not always) more complex, they may take longer to complete. Even if they are long-term projects, you will most likely see organizational improvement along the way.

The reason for emphasizing projects with a high chance for success is to get more people behind the transformation process as early as possible. Organizational transformation is really the psychological and sociological transformation of people and teams. Because people like success, you will get support more quickly if you can achieve success early in the process.

If you have a strategic planning process, assure that the projects related to transformation feed into it or are a part of it. If you don't align the transformation with strategic planning, people will become confused regarding what to work on and what is important to the organization.

The Affinity Diagram

A very simple and effective method for organizing a group of items is the Affinity Diagram. The Affinity Diagram is created by writing each item on a separate removable note sheet (for example, a Post-It® Note) and placing it on a wall or white board in a random order. As each note is placed on the wall, it is discussed to assure everyone on the team understands its meaning and relationship to the company's culture and operation and the overall objective of transformation. Once all of the items are on the wall, a time limit is set to complete the grouping of the items (the amount of time depends on the number of items, but 15 minutes is generally sufficient). As the grouping process begins, team members move the notes around to put similar items together. This is done without talking to avoid slowing down the process. If one team member thinks two items are similar, he or she puts them together on the wall. If another disagrees, he or she separates them without discussion. This form of silent arguing will go back and forth until someone gives up or the time limit expires.

Once the time limit has passed, everyone sits down and the groupings are discussed in an effort to identify the overall theme of each group of items. The themes identified will become the project titles, and the individual items under each can become components (or sub-projects) of the initiatives (see Figure 8.2).

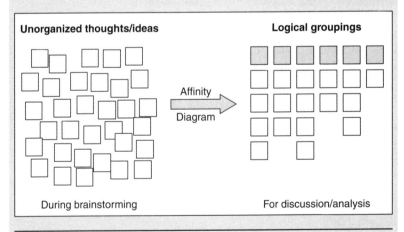

Figure 8.2 The affinity diagram.

Have Fun

A very simple truth in virtually any endeavor is that people do a better job if they are enjoying what they are doing. If you make the workplace fun, people will miss fewer days, be more willing to contribute, and be less likely to leave if a higher-paying job comes along.

A factory worker at a U.S. Toyota plant once told me that he liked working for the company so much that he would be willing to do his job for less money. That one statement tells more about the company than any stock analysis or financial report could.

Making the workplace fun does not mean hiring stand-up comics or clowns to entertain workers. It means creating an environment where people want to spend their time. A fun environment is one where people:

- Feel respected by fellow employees and leaders

- Are listened to when making suggestions or raising concerns

- Contribute to an unchanging cause that they believe in

- Are proud to be associated with

- Continually learn and grow

- Believe in their leaders and trust their intentions

These are all simple but extremely powerful elements of a healthy organization. Transformation is not an easy or quick process. It is, however, a journey that can be psychologically and financially rewarding for those who are truly ready to initiate the process. The first requirement is to understand that you have problems that need attention. The second requirement is to realize that your organization can be transformed to enter the group of the few elite companies that are feared and envied by their competitors, and highly valued by their customers.

NOTES

[1] Bernarnos, Georges. 1968. "France Before the World of Tomorrow." *The Last Essays of Georges Bernarnos.* Portsmouth, NH: Greenwood Press.

Appendix A

Internal Organizational Assessment

The intent of the organizational assessment that follows is to determine the existence and extent of the warning signs of organizational decline. There is no magic formula for removing the warning signs, and just knowing that you have them is not going to make the situation improve. For improvement to occur, the leaders need to understand and validate the existence of the warnings, believe they can and need to be removed, and truly desire to remove them.

The first step is to understand which warning signs are present within your organization and reflect to determine the fundamental reasons for their existence. Some of the warning signs will be easy to eliminate (for example, if you have a performance evaluation system, you stop using it), while others will require a fundamental change in the organization (for example, refocusing the attention of people on a common purpose of the organization).

The results of the assessment require a dialogue between the people within the organization to agree that the warning signs exist and that they are problems that will interfere with present or future success. In some cases, employees will need to be surveyed to some degree to provide objective answers.

PRIORITIZING ACTION

Determining where to begin the process of organizational transformation can be overwhelming. To help with the process, each response in the assessment has been assigned a weighting factor to prioritize areas of the organization needing attention. The numbers are only to be used as a general guideline, however, and should not be blindly followed. The management team should discuss the results and come to a consensus regarding where to begin. If the team feels they will be more successful by addressing an area

138 *Appendix A*

that does not end up with the highest score, they should follow their instincts. The objective is continual improvement and as long as this is occurring, the team is doing its job.

To determine the factor for each of the warning signs, calculate the average response for the questions in that section (that is, add the numbers for the selected responses for the section and divide by the number of non-N/A responses). For example, if the section contains 10 assessment questions and eight are considered applicable, the numbers associated with the eight responses are added and the total is divided by eight.

Although the objective of determining the warning sign factor is to determine which is the most glaring for the company for prioritization of improvement efforts, the biggest benefit of the exercise is the analysis process itself.

		Degree of Existence			
Sign 1 Lost Focus		Hi	Mod	Lo	N/A
1-1	The purpose of the organization is clear and well understood by everyone	③	④	⑤	☐
1-2	The purpose is focused on the need the organization provides to its customers, rather than financial motives	③	④	⑤	☐
1-3	The purpose is defined in terms of fulfilling a need instead of a product or product type	③	④	⑤	☐
1-4	People within the organization view the mission statement as inspiring, and feel proud to strive for its achievement	③	④	⑤	☐
1-5	People and departments within the organization work toward optimizing the performance of the organization as a whole, rather than on individual or department goals which conflict with each other	③	④	⑤	☐
1-6	The purpose of the organization has remained constant over the last several years	③	④	⑤	☐
1-7	Effort is made during the hiring process to assure that job candidates understand the purpose, and are eager to be a part of its achievement	③	④	⑤	☐
1-8	Customers would suffer if the company went out of business	③	④	⑤	☐

Internal Organizational Assessment   **139**

	Degree of Existence			
	Hi	Mod	Lo	N/A
1-9 Competitors respect the company's capabilities and performance	③	④	⑤	☐

Lost Focus:

Sum total of responses = _____ ÷ Applicable Questions = _____

Sign 2 Number Obsession

		Hi	Mod	Lo	N/A
2-1	Meetings start with operational issues rather than discussions of financial measures	①	②	③	☐
2-2	During management meetings, as much (or more) time is spent discussing people, systems, and operational issues as financial matters	①	②	③	☐
2-3	Management uses a variety of measures to understand performance, including customer, quality, cycle time/delivery, and other non-financially based indicators	①	②	③	☐
2-4	Key measures are displayed as graphs with clear definitions of what is being measured (that is, operational definitions) and control limits to help people truly understand what the data means	①	②	③	☐
2-5	Managers within the company are trained in statistical methods, and understand the meaning of control limits	①	②	③	☐
2-6	There is no extra focus at the end of periods (months, quarters, and so on) on meeting shipping, revenue, or other financial targets	①	②	③	☐
2-7	On-time delivery to customer requirements is more important to management than the number of dollars shipped	①	②	③	☐
2-8	The need to cut costs and/or reduce budgets due to a drop in sales or profits is rare	①	②	③	☐
2-9	The management team is comprised of more technical professionals than financial professionals	①	②	③	☐

Number Obsession:

Sum total of responses = _____ ÷ Applicable Questions = _____

140 *Appendix A*

		Degree of Existence			
Sign 3 Supplier Squeezing		Hi	Mod	Lo	N/A
3-1	The focus of purchasing professionals within the company is to reduce the total cost of incoming materials and services, rather than just the price	①	②	③	☐
3-2	Management understands the importance of the total cost of purchased materials, supplies, and services	①	②	③	☐
3-3	The turnover of suppliers is continually reduced in favor of long-term relationships	①	②	③	☐
3-4	Efforts are aimed at continually reducing the supplier base for the purchase of key products, materials, and services	①	②	③	☐
3-5	Reducing the total cost of procurement is the responsibility of more than just the purchasing department	①	②	③	☐
3-6	The quality of purchased materials, supplies, and services is reported to suppliers on a regular basis in an effort to continually improve	①	②	③	☐
3-7	Suppliers are paid under terms that assure that they are successful and remain profitable and benefit both the organization and the supplier	①	②	③	☐
3-8	Purchasing professionals regularly talk with the people inside the organization who use the products and services they purchase to assure the users are satisfied	①	②	③	☐
3-9	The organization provides technical support to suppliers to help them continually improve the products and services they provide	①	②	③	☐
3-10	Suppliers are involved in the new product/service development process	①	②	③	☐
3-11	Suppliers are surveyed regularly to determine how easy the organization (as the customer) is to do business with	①	②	③	☐
3-12	Supplier selection is done with a clear understanding of the needs of users	①	②	③	☐

Supplier Squeezing:

    Sum total of responses = _____ ÷ Applicable Questions = _____

Internal Organizational Assessment 141

Sign 4 Undervalued Employees	Degree of Existence			
	Hi	Mod	Lo	N/A
4-1 The organization does not lay off workers on a regular basis to respond to drops in sales or other financial performance measures	①	②	③	☐
4-2 Employee satisfaction surveys are conducted regularly, and the results used as input for management and organizational improvement efforts	①	②	③	☐
4-3 A high percentage of employees participate in employee satisfaction surveys	①	②	③	☐
4-4 Employee satisfaction continually improves	①	②	③	☐
4-5 The fear of making mistakes is not a prevalent attitude within the company	①	②	③	☐
4-6 Management has voluntarily forfeited their bonuses in any year when layoffs have taken place	①	②	③	☐
4-7 The company does not utilize a traditional performance review process	①	②	③	☐
4-8 The objective of a performance feedback process is to improve, and is accompanied by a documented personal improvement plan based on the feedback received	①	②	③	☐
4-9 The feedback process utilized by the company (whether it is a traditional review, 360° review, or some other type of process) is not tied to pay increases or bonuses	①	②	③	☐
4-10 The feedback process allows the person receiving the feedback to keep the results personal and confidential	①	②	③	☐
4-11 A significant percentage of management personnel within the company were developed from within the organization	①	②	③	☐
4-12 People within the organization are required to spend enough time in a given position to learn the job well before being considered for another position	①	②	③	☐

142 *Appendix A*

		Degree of Existence			
		Hi	Mod	Lo	N/A
4-13	There is a formal process within the organization to assure that people are trained in a consistent and effective manner	①	②	③	☐
4-14	There is a formal hiring process that focuses on the candidate's values and ability to fit into the company's culture, at least as much as his or her technical capabilities	①	②	③	☐
4-15	Fear of layoffs or firings is not prevalent within the company	①	②	③	☐
4-16	People do not fear questioning management decisions or actions that they do not understand	①	②	③	☐

Undervalued Employees:
 Sum total of responses = _____ ÷ Applicable Questions = _____

Sign 5 Dirt, Clutter, and Damage

5-1	The organization's machines and equipment are well maintained, don't break down often, and don't exhibit signs of wear and tear	①	②	③	☐
5-2	Old or broken down machines and equipment are not replaced without first understanding the cause of the deterioration or damage	①	②	③	☐
5-3	The company uses a preventive maintenance system to maintain machines and equipment, and does not compromise the system in response to fluctuating business conditions	①	②	③	☐
5-4	A clean workplace is valued within the organization and the cleanliness is continually improved	①	②	③	☐
5-5	Time is set aside every day to allow people to clean the workplace	①	②	③	☐
5-6	People regularly use work slowdowns as opportunities to clean the workplace	①	②	③	☐
5-7	The company uses a formalized process for organizing and cleaning the workplace	①	②	③	☐

		Degree of Existence		
		Hi	Mod	Lo	N/A

5-8 Machines and equipment that are used for measurement are calibrated regularly — ① ② ③ ☐

Dirt, Clutter, and Damage:
   Sum total of responses = _____ ÷ Applicable Questions = _____

Sign 6 Operational Fragmentation

6-1 People in the company generally focus on overall organizational performance, rather than individual or department goals — ① ② ③ ☐

6-2 The organization is not managed as individual profit centers — ① ② ③ ☐

6-3 Actions are focused on optimizing the overall system instead of individual function areas or business units — ① ② ③ ☐

6-4 Salespeople within the company are not paid on a commission basis — ① ② ③ ☐

6-5 The physical layout of the people within the company is based on processes, products, or services rather than functions — ① ② ③ ☐

6-6 New products and services are developed through a team approach involving representatives from all relevant functions — ① ② ③ ☐

6-7 Suppliers are involved in the development of new products or services — ① ② ③ ☐

6-8 The management team understands the process for creating and delivering the products and/or services delivered to customers (including the flow of materials and information) — ① ② ③ ☐

6-9 Management is not overly focused on measuring the performance of individuals — ③ ④ ⑤ ☐

6-10 Bonuses are based on overall company performance instead of individual, team, or business unit performance — ③ ④ ⑤ ☐

6-11 The strategic planning process is based on continually improving the company's system — ③ ④ ⑤ ☐

Operational Fragmentation
   Sum total of responses = _____ ÷ Applicable Questions = _____

144 *Appendix A*

WARNING SIGN PRIORITIZATION

Plot the results of the assessment on the chart below by shading the average score for each warning sign in an effort to prioritize areas in need of improvement.

	Sign 1 Lost Focus	Sign 2 Number Obsession	Sign 3 Supplier Squeezing	Sign 4 Undervalued Employees	Sign 5 Dirt and Clutter	Sign 6 Operation Fragment
5.0						
3.5						
3.0						
2.5						
2.0						
1.5						
1.0						
0.5						
0						

Appendix B
Statistical Process Control

Developed by Walter Shewhart in the 1920s, Statistical Process Control (SPC) uses some very basic formulas and simple rules to understand whether or not a system is stable (that is, is operating as it was designed). In a stable system, any improvement desired must come from a redesign of the system (usually requiring management involvement and participation by persons from a variety of areas of the organization).

Shewhart's method uses the average and range to calculate what he termed *control limits*. The control limits are estimates of the value for three standard deviations (or 3σ) on each side of the average for a measured characteristic, which should represent 99.73% of the results of the system. In general, as long as the numbers follow random patterns within the control limits (meaning that no identifiable patterns emerge, as defined in the rules presented later in this appendix and shown in Figure B.1), the system is considered stable, and improvement will only come from a fundamental change in the system's design.

Using SPC, control limits can be calculated with as little as 15 data points, instead of 100–150, which are required to construct a histogram (to determine a picture of the actual distribution). This can also be done using historical data if available rather than waiting 15 periods for data to be collected.

The relevance of SPC to leading an organization is related to the analysis of key measures used by leaders. Without SPC, it is virtually impossible to fully understand what the indicators are truly saying about the organization, how to approach improvement, and how the organization is capable of performing with its present systems. Managers do not need to be experts in SPC to understand data, but they do need to have a basic understanding of the rules of variation.

Because statistics is not the focus of this book, the information provided in this appendix is kept to a very basic level. Further and more

146 *Appendix B*

in-depth information can be obtained from a number of excellent books published on the subject.

THE BASIC STATISTICAL FORMULAS

The formulas below are intended to be used with data commonly collected for key organization measures (that is, on-time delivery, warranty expenses, and so on). They assume that only one point is collected per period (that is, sample size is one) and that a two-period moving average is calculated. For information regarding formulas for different circumstances, refer to textbooks on the subject of statistical process control.

After collecting at least 12 data points, create a run chart (line graph) of the information, and perform the following steps:

Step 1: Calculate Moving Range (n=2)

The difference between each pair of values in the order they are collected (that is, if the first value is 74.3 and the second value is 78.1, the moving range is $78.1 - 74.3 = 3.8$. If the third value is 76.0, the moving range is $78.1 - 76.0 = 2.1$). The moving range is always a positive number, and the difference between each successive data point (as a new data point is added, the first is dropped). Because in this example n=2, the moving range is the difference between two successive measurements, there will always be one less range than data points (that is, there will not be a range for the first data point).

Step 2: Calculate Average

Add the data points together and divide by the number of data points (that is, if the data points are 5, 5, 6, 7, 8, 3, 9, 8, 4, 6, 5, 5, then the average is $[5 + 5 + 6 + 7 + 8 + 3 + 9 + 8 + 4 + 6 + 5 + 5] / 12 = 71 / 12 = 5.92$). Draw a line in the chart to represent the average. The average is represented as $\bar{X}$ (referred to as *x bar*).

Step 3: Calculate the Average Moving Range

The moving range average is the sum of the moving range values, divided by the number of moving range values. The moving range is represented by $\bar{R}$ (referred to as *r bar*).

Step 4: Plot Individual Values

Draw a line graph representing the individual values collected each period.

Step 5: Calculate the Control Limits

Control limits represent the values that can be expected to fall within 3σ (standard deviations) from the average. This represents 99.73% (or virtually all) of the values for the measure.

The control limits are calculated as follows:

$$\text{Upper Control Limit (UCL)} = \bar{X} + 2.66\bar{R}$$

$$\text{Lower Control Limit (LCL)} = \bar{X} - 2.66\bar{R}$$

Draw the control limits on the chart, and use the rules (presented in Figure B.2) to determine whether or not the data represent a stable distribution.

RULES TO DETERMINE STABILITY OF A SYSTEM

The basic rules to determine whether a system is stable have appeared in a number of books and articles on the subject of statistical process control. Although there are some differences in the presentation of the rules in publications, they all basically test for the same thing: a nonrandom pattern of data based on the probability of occurrence.

Since the rules first appeared in the Western Electric Statistical Quality Control Handbook[1] (Bonnie B. Small, Chairman of the Writing Committee, Western Electric Company, Indianapolis, 1956), they are often referred to as the *Western Electric Rules*, although there have been clarifications and additions to the rules since they were first published.

1. *Any point outside of the control limits.* Because there is only a 0.27% chance that a value will fall outside of a control limit, any occurrence is considered to represent a lack of stability.

2. *Two out of three successive points fall outside of the 2σ limits* (that is, greater than ± 2 standard deviations from average, even though they may be inside the 3σ limits). The 2σ limits can be calculated by multiplying the control limits by 0.667.

3. *Four out of five successive points fall outside of the 1σ limits* (that is, greater than ± 1 standard deviation from the average, even though they may be inside the 3σ limits). The 1σ limits can be calculated by multiplying the control limits by 0.333.

148 Appendix B

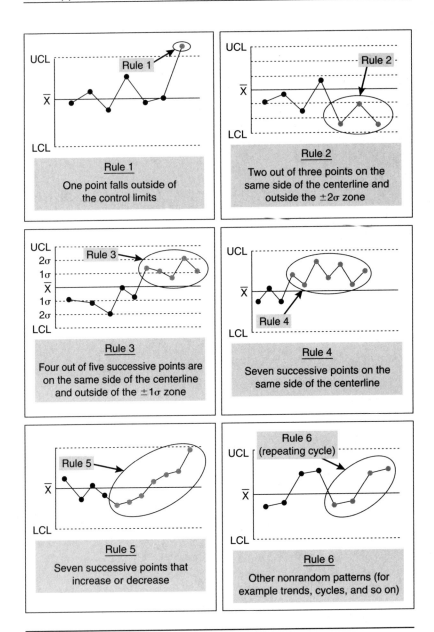

Figure B.1 Charts depicting data from unstable systems.

4. *Seven consecutive points on the same side of the center line* (that is, above or below the average). Because this represents a non-random pattern, it is believed to be the result of an unstable system.

5. *Seven consecutive points increasing or decreasing.* As with Rule 4 (above), this represents a pattern and is, therefore considered non-random (or unstable).

6. *Any other non-random pattern* (that is, trends, cycles, or other recognizable pattern).

NOTES

[1] Small, Bonnie B. 1956. *Western Electric Statistical Quality Control Handbook.* Indianapolis, IN: Western Electric Company.

Appendix C

The QFD Process

Quality Function Deployment (QFD) is a process to bring together all functions in the organization to focus on a single objective: meeting the voice of the customer. Most commonly used in product or service development, the process uses a series of matrices to assure that customer needs are considered throughout the entire process by involving persons from a variety of functional areas.

Only brief explanations of each step are given because this is not meant to be a text on the QFD process. If more information is desired, there are several good books available on the subject.

The key to success with QFD is to assure that all affected areas are represented throughout the project to make use of the level of expertise within the organization (Figure C.1 shows the level of involvement of the more common functional areas in each step for a typical product development project). Figure C.2 presents an example of a QFD matrix for the development of a tennis racquet. Refer to Figure C.2 to better understand the steps provided below.

The steps in the QFD process are as follows:

1. Determine project objective. In order to assure the people on the development team have a clear understanding of their task, and that it is consistent with the expectations of management. The objective also provides the team with the expected deliverable(s) for the project.

2. Set project scope. The scope of the project lets the team know what the boundaries of the project are: for example, what they can and cannot do. The scope also provides the expected completion date for the project.

3. Determine customer requirements. Customer requirements are collected by asking the customers for their requirements for the product or service being developed. The key here is to dig down below the surface of what the customers are telling you to know what their fundamental needs are. Often, customers do not know what is possible and only express what

151

they want in terms of what they have been given by you and your competitors in the past, rather than their true needs (for example, does a customer want a car that gets up to 40 mpg or that is high in fuel efficiency to reduce fuel expenses?).

Customer interviews, focus groups, surveys, observation of the product or service in use, warranty records, and complaints are all useful for this step.

4. Categorize customer requirements. To enable the team to organize the information gathered in the previous step. This allows the team to begin to focus its efforts in the project. An affinity diagram is a very commonly used tool during this stage in the project (see Chapter 8 for an explanation of the Affinity Diagram).

5. Prioritize customer requirements. Customer requirements need to be prioritized so the team can spend its time only on those requirements that are most important to the customer. Often, this step requires a survey of customers to let them select the most important aspects of the product or service. The requirements are prioritized by assigning a numeric value between one and five.

6. Assess competitive position. To further focus the project on the most important aspects of the product or service under development, the competitive position of the product or service characteristics needs to be determined. Assessing competitive position involves asking the customers how well you and competitors are meeting the need at the present time. The objectives are to understand the requirements that are important, but are not being satisfied by you or your competitors, and to determine which company is best serving the customer at the present time. This information should be gathered from the survey conducted during the previous step.

7. Develop design requirements. The team needs to determine which technical product or service characteristics relate to each customer requirement. For example, if the team is developing a tennis racquet, and comfortable grip is one of the characteristics deemed to be important by the team, then the team may determine that the technical characteristics that affect the comfort of the grip include varied grip sizes, compression, grip length, and grip material (which includes texture, absorbency, and thickness).

A cause and effect diagram can be very useful in this step, placing the customer requirement as the "cause," and determining the technical requirements as the "effects."

8. Determine relationships. Relationships are determined by comparing each technical requirement against each customer requirement to determine the strength of the relationship. This step in the process is intended to make sure customer requirements are addressed in the product or service technical specifications. Relationships are signified with a symbol in the cell of the intersecting row (customer requirement) and column (technical requirement) to make the matrix more visual and easy to read. Although any symbol can be used, the most common are a triangle (Δ) for weak relationships, a circle (○) for moderate relationships, and a double circle (◉) for strong relationships. If there is no relationship, the cell is left blank.

9. Perform a competitive assessment. A competitive assessment is performed on the technical requirements to help the team focus its efforts on those technical requirements that are in the most need of improvement. The key of this step is to identify the technical requirements that relate to key customer requirements where customers feel that nobody is performing well or where a competitor is performing well and you are not. This assessment is performed by the entire team because it involves a technical assessment to compare specifications of your product or service with that of the competition.

10. Set target values. Target values for the product or service characteristics are determined based on the level of importance from the previous step. At this stage, only preliminary target values are set because they may change later in the project after further analysis is performed.

11. Define technical requirement weights. Weights for the technical requirements are defined to further narrow the focus of the team; weights are calculated for each of the technical requirements. To calculate the weights for each technical requirement, multiply the relationship value (1 for weak-Δ; 3 for moderate-○, and 9 for strong-◉) from Step 8 by the importance value of the customer requirement it is related to, and add up the results. For example, in the tennis racquet example shown in Figure C.2, grip material has a moderate relationship to low stress on elbow (which has an importance value of 4), a strong relationship to comfortable grip (importance value of 3), a moderate value for easy to handle (importance value of 3), and a weak relationship to

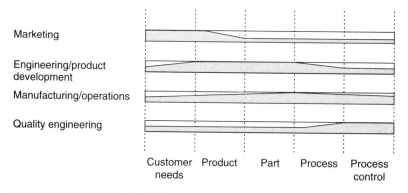

Figure C.1 Level of involvement/leadership at each step of the process.

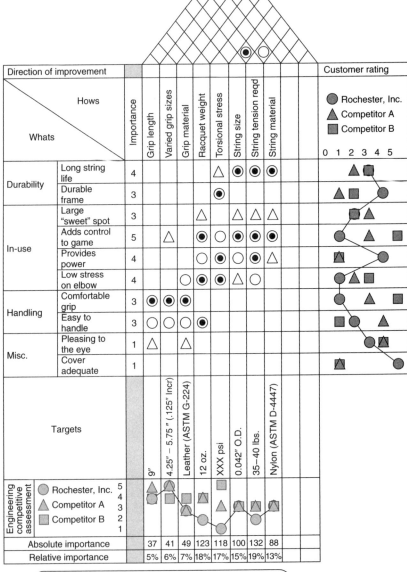

Figure C.2 QFD matrix example.[1]

pleasing to the eye (importance value of 1), then the weight for grip material would be:

$$(3 \times 4) + (9 \times 3) + (3 \times 3) + (1 \times 1) = 49$$

The same type of calculation would be done for each technical requirement to determine which are the most important.

Determining weights based on relationships forces the team to focus its efforts on those technical specifications which have the greatest effect on fundamental customer needs. This prevents wasting effort on those aspects that the customer considers to be less important.

12. Analyze technical requirement correlations. Technical requirements are correlated by comparing the technical requirements against each other to determine whether they are correlated. This becomes the roof of the matrix in Figure C.2, and requires technical knowledge of the product or service characteristics. The objective here is to understand the effect of improving one technical characteristic on the others. If improving one characteristic automatically improves another, the correlation is positive (identified by a double-cross if the correlation is strong, and a single cross if it is merely positive). If improving a characteristic negatively impacts another characteristic, the correlation is negative (signified by a double circle for strong negative correlations and an open circle for negative correlations).

The main purpose for this exercise is to determine where problems will exist in meeting customer needs in a product or service because of physics or cost considerations. If trade-offs need to be made between customer requirements, then it is better to make the choice consciously early in the project than to face it later in the process.

13. Finalize target values. The target values for technical characteristics are finalized after the correlations are determined.

14. Deploy information to other matrices. Once the product or service characteristics have been finalized (by completing the initial matrix), the information can be deployed to the other matrices. The other matrices commonly include Part Characteristics Matrix (to address individual part characteristics), Process Characteristics Matrix (to identify the process characteristics necessary to meet customer needs), and the Process Control Matrix (to determine the level and types of controls to be applied within the process to assure customer requirements are met). See Figure C.3 for a visual depiction of the QFD process.

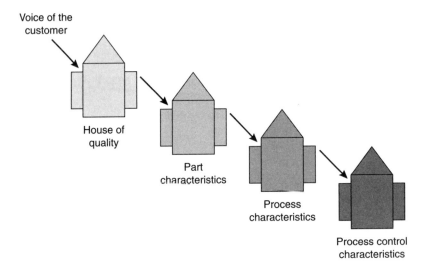

Figure C.3 Overview of the QFD process.

NOTES

[1] Stocker, Gregg. 1991."Quality Function Deployment: Using the Voice of the Customer." *APICS: The Performance Advantage* 1:3.

Appendix D

Basic Reflection Questions

The following questions are best answered by a team of managers with the authority to make changes in the organization. There is no need to answer all questions. Select the questions that most closely relate to the culture, environment, and personalities within the organization. They are meant to get the team to reflect on fundamental problems that may be so engrained in the organization that they have become an accepted mode of operation.

Reflection is a necessary component of organizational and personal learning. Learning will not occur, however, if the discussion is not followed up with actions to improve the organization.

1. Is profit the cause or effect of a successful organization? Explain. Where does your organization place its focus? Where should it focus?

2. Do you feel that your organization's purpose needs to include a reference to profitability? Do you think that people would not think profit is important if your purpose did not include it? Why or why not? What effect does a reference to profit in your mission statement have?

3. Does the mission statement of your organization describe why the organization exists and what value it provides to society? Is the statement something that makes you proud to be associated with the company?

4. Does everyone in your organization understand the organization's purpose? Would it help the people in your organization be more effective if they understood the purpose of the organization? How should the purpose be communicated throughout the organization? What could you do to help others understand the organization's purpose?

5. Do you have a passion for the purpose of your organization? How important is it for people to have a passion for the organization's purpose? Do the people within the organization have a passion for the purpose? Why or why not? What can you do to improve the situation?

6. What are the objectives of your department? Are they aligned with those of the organization? Is it possible for you to achieve your objectives in a way that will interfere with the ability of others to achieve theirs? If so, why? What should you do about it?

7. Have you ever identified your role in helping other departments achieve their objectives? Do you have any incentive to do so?

8. Who are your customers within the organization? Do you know how they use your services to do their jobs? Have you ever asked them how well you are serving their needs and how you could improve the level of service you provide to them? If not, should you? Are any needs of your internal customers addressed in your personal or departmental objectives?

9. Who are your suppliers within the organization? Have you ever discussed with them how they could help you better serve your customers? Would they be receptive to such a discussion? Why or why not? What should you do?

10. What are the barriers within the organization to having the types of conversations referred to in questions 8 and 9? Who is responsible for removing those barriers and how might it be done?

11. What are the things that the people in the organization fear the most? How can the fear be reduced or eliminated?

12. Is your boss your customer? Is it more important for someone to please his or her boss than the customer? Does pleasing the boss ever interfere with pleasing the customer? Is it possible for someone in your organization to think that pleasing his or her boss is more important than pleasing the customer? If so, why is this happening and what can be done to improve the situation?

13. If your organization has multiple facilities, can there be a situation where one facility is profitable while it is actually

Basic Reflection Questions   159

hurting the rest of the organization? Can the situation be improved? How?

14. Are the people within your organization open to accepting help from people at other facilities? Why or why not? Can you identify any barriers to this type of sharing and support that may have been created by management philosophy, behaviors, or actions? What should be done to remove the barriers, whether or not they have been created by management?

15. If your organization has multiple facilities, do they share information between each other to facilitate improvement? Does your culture (and the personalities of the facility managers) interfere with sharing information between locations?

16. Does the way in which your organization measures individual facilities interfere with success of the organization as a whole? Can an individual facility meet its objectives without helping the organization?

17. What are the potential problems for an organization and its leaders in moving from short-term to long-term thinking? How should the leaders handle the shift to long-term focus?

18. Does your organization have the technical knowledge to be successful with continual improvement? Does it have the culture that will enable continual improvement to be successful? Which is more important? If both need improvement, which should be addressed first?

19. What problems could it cause for your organization if you moved the purchases of a critical component or material to a single supplier? What could the benefits be? If you decided to move to single sourcing for a critical component, what would you need to do to make it happen?

20. Are you happy with your suppliers? Are they happy with you? Is it important for them to be happy with you? Should you do anything to improve the situation?

21. Are there any barriers within the organization that will interfere with defragmenting the organization? If so, clearly define each barrier and prioritize in terms of significance. What would it take to begin to remove the highest priority barriers?

Glossary

5S—a method for gaining control of a dirty and unorganized workplace. The five steps to the process (all starting with the letter S) include Sort, Scrub, Setup, Standardize, Sustain.

control cycle—a cycle of management that breaks down (or continues to break down) trust, innovation, and motivation of workers. The cycle begins with management's distrust of employees' intentions and abilities. Through a high level of control and a series of actions and behaviors on the part of management, the cycle results in creating an environment where employees lose ambition and don't contribute to improvement.

corporate death spiral—a continual decline in the size and financial strength of an organization due to decisions and actions that are focused on short-term improvement at the expense of long-term performance.

crisis-mode management—a series of actions taken by managers in response to a drop in business or profits that are directed at short-term improvement in a company's financial position (for example, layoffs, pay cuts, elimination of benefits, and so on).

dirt, clutter, and damage—a warning sign of organizational decline that consists of a workplace that is dirty and/or unorganized, and buildings, property, and equipment that are not properly maintained.

fundamental change—a shift in deeply held beliefs about people, business, and society that results in a long-term change in behavior.

headcount—the number of people on the payroll at a given point in time.

heavy losses—a phrase coined by W. Edwards Deming referring to the things that cause the greatest losses for an organization. According to Deming, these are the things that cannot be measured, but must be managed and continually improved by management (for example, the

162 *Glossary*

reduction of fear, improvement of morale and motivation of employees, improvements of customer satisfaction, and so on).

in-control—a process or system that is stable and produces statistically consistent and predictable results.

lost focus—forgetting why the company exists, resulting in people focusing on personal definitions of success (which often conflict with each other and are heavily financially driven).

mission—the fundamental reason for an organization's existence. It is a definition of the value that the organization provides to its customers.

number obsession—a warning sign of organizational decline that consists of focusing heavily on financial indicators while paying little or no attention to the non-measurable aspects of a business (for example, morale, culture, leadership development, and so on).

operational fragmentation—a warning sign of organizational decline that occurs when the level of teamwork is low and the company is operated as a fragmented group of departments and people instead of as a single system working together to accomplish a common purpose.

parent poisoning—an occurrence in mergers and acquisitions when the parent company forgets its reason for existence (its mission) because of the merger and is poisoned by the sick culture of the purchased company.

purpose—a organization's mission (why it is in business) and vision (where it is headed).

quality function deployment (QFD)—project-management tool that brings together all relevant functions in the organization to focus on the single objective of meeting the voice of the customer. QFD uses a series of matrices to translate the voice of the customer into specific, actionable steps for the team.

stability (process or system)—a state that is achieved when data collected from a process or system show statistically predictable patterns.

statistical process control (SPC)—tool that uses basic statistical formulas to determine the stability of a process or system.

supplier squeezing—a warning sign of organizational decline that results when management does not value the relationship with suppliers and focuses procurement efforts on reducing the price of incoming products and services instead of working toward a long-term mutually beneficial relationship to improve quality, cost, and delivery.

supplier turnover—the percentage of an organization's suppliers that are changed over a given period of time (that is, the number of new suppliers divided by the total number of suppliers for a given period).

Glossary 163

systems thinking—focusing on the performance and operation of the system as a whole instead of the individual components.

total cost—the total costs to the organization of a particular component of the business. Consists of looking beyond those costs that are easy to measure and includes aspects like delays, customer satisfaction and employee issues, and costs incurred in parts of the organization away from the immediate area of the aspect being measured.

undervalued employees—a warning sign of organizational decline that occurs when leaders do not place a high value on employees. Layoffs are common, fear is prevalent, and there is very little leadership development within the organization. Attempts are made to measure employee performance without taking into account nonmeasurable contributions.

vision—the component of purpose that defines where the organization is headed in the future.

warning signs—indicators of the practices that lead an organization into decline and, when one or more negative external events occurs, can result in the organization entering a death spiral.

Index

A

acquisitions, 21–23
affinity diagram, 134
assessment
  of organization, 132–133, 137–144
  of organizational purpose, 20, 133
  of product position, 152
  of technical requirements, 153
atomistic management, 99
automotive industry suppliers, 60

B

balanced scorecard, 30
Berkshire-Hathaway, 42
Bethune, Gordon, 21
Boeing, 19, 20
bonuses
  as clue to fragmentation, 121
  inappropriate bases for, 33, 100–102
  layoffs and, 67–68
  problems caused by, 103, 110
bosses, contrasted with leaders, 10
budgeting expenses, 101–102
Built to Last (Collins & Porras), 13–14
business cycles, 12

C

candidates, job. *See* job seekers
capitalization, market, 12
CD (compact disc) technology, 24, 25
change, fundamental, 161. *See also*
  transformation, business
cluttered work environments. *See* work
  environments, dirty/disorganized

coach, leader role as, 127
Coca-Cola, 42
Collins, James, 13
commissions, sales, 114–117
compact disc (CD) technology, 24, 25
comparisons between
  department/operation, 33–34, 76–77
compensation, 33, 43. *See also* bonuses
competition, intra-company, 33–34, 76–77
competitive assessment of technical
  requirements, 153
competitive position of product, 152
Continental Airlines, 21
continual improvement, 56–57, 67
control cycle, defined, 161
control limits, 145
corporate death spiral, defined, 161. *See
  also* organizational decline
costs
  cutting, 4
  immeasurable, 30
  supplier-associated, 49
  total, 45–49, 50–51, 55, 163
creativity, 80
crisis-mode management, 4, 161
culture, company
  supportive, 5–6
  toxic. *See* organizational decline
customers
  confidence of, 91, 93
  focus on, 12, 14
  identifying, 52–54
  requirements of, 151–152
  satisfaction of, 23–24, 30–31
cutbacks, 6–7

166 *Index*

D

damaged work environments. *See* work
  environments, dirty/disorganized
deadlines, product development, 100
death spiral. *See* organizational decline
Define-Measure-Analyze-Improve-Control
  (DMAIC) approach, 103
Deming, W. Edwards
  on employee fear, 79
  on goal-setting, 104
  influence on Japanese business, 113
  on organizational costs, 30
  on organizational purpose, 16
  on performance evaluations, 70
  on systems thinking, 50
departments
  competitions between, 33–34, 76–77
  fragmentation of. *See* fragmentation,
    departmental
design requirements, 152–153, 155
development
  employee, 14, 23, 75–78, 81
  personal, 128
  product, 100
  supplier, 57–58, 121
dirty/disorganized work environments. *See*
  work environments,
  dirty/disorganized
DMAIC (Define-Measure-Analyze-
  Improve-Control) approach, 103

E

earnings estimates. *See* forecasts, financial
ego, leader, 9, 10
employee development, 14, 23, 75–78, 81
employees. *See also* layoffs, employee;
  performance evaluations;
  undervaluing employees
  fear, 78–80, 127, 132
  focus on, 9, 10, 12
  identifying departmental fragmentation,
    118, 120–121
  identifying financial obsession, 43
  identifying lack of
    cleanliness/organization, 97
  identifying lack of organizational
    purpose, 26
  identifying supplier squeezing, 58–59
  identifying undervaluing of employees,
    80–82

motivation of, 2–3, 17, 19
  performance, factors affecting, 119
  satisfaction, 30
  teamwork, 30, 76–77, 109–112
  turnover, 30, 82
equipment/machine problems, detecting,
  93–94
estimated earnings. *See* forecasts,
  financial
expenses, budgeting/reducing, 65–66,
  101–102
extrinsic motivation, 17

F

facility opening dates, 102
fear
  employee, 78–80, 127, 132
  management, 9
The Fifth Discipline (Senge), 50
financial indicators, focus on
  benefits, 31
  costs, 21, 31–34, 44, 125
  defined, 29, 162
  forecasting. *See* forecasts, financial
  halting excess, 34–35
  identifying, 29–30, 43–44
  overview, 7–8
  reasons for, 11–12
Five Whys, 129–132
5S process, 94–97, 161
focus, business. *See* purpose,
  organizational
Ford, Henry, 18–19, 20
Ford Motor Company, 20
forecasts
  financial, 42
  sales, 101
  shipping, 100–101
Fourth Generation Management (Joiner),
  42
fragmentation, departmental
  causes, 109–112
  costs, 100–102, 109–112, 114–116
  defined, 8, 99, 162
  factors encouraging, 114–117
  goal-setting and, 104
  identifying, 118, 120–121
  reducing, 112–113
fun work environments, 135
fundamental change, defined, 161

G

Gallery Furniture, 8
Galvin, Robert, 32
Gillette, 42
goals, 99–102, 104–109. *See also* PDSA
Google, 19, 20
grades as evaluative tool, 76–77
guided reflection, 129–132

H

headcount, defined, 161
heavy losses, 30, 161–162
Hewlett-Packard, 44
Hillerich & Bradsby, 2, 8, 79–80
Hillerich, Jack, III, 79–80
hiring, 66–67, 78, 116
Honda, 26
House of Quality matrix, 154, 156

I

improvement, continual, 56–57, 67
improvement initiatives, failure of, 6, 66
in-control systems, 36–37, 145, 147, 162
independent profit centers, 16–17, 120–121
innovation, 80
Internet, purchasing via, 54–55
intrinsic motivation, 17
inventory control, 93, 94, 103
investors
  cutting dividends to, 64–65, 67
  goals/values, 12, 14–16
  identifying companies that undervalue
    employees, 82–83
  identifying departmental fragmentation,
    121
  identifying financial obsession, 43–44
  identifying lack of
    cleanliness/organization, 98
  identifying purposeless organizations,
    27
  identifying supplier squeezing, 59–60
  mission statements and, 19–20
IQ, 77

J

Japan, business rise of, 113
job cuts. *See* layoffs, employee
job seekers
  identifying departmental fragmentation,
    121

identifying employee undervaluing,
    82–83
identifying financial obsession, 43
identifying lack of
    cleanliness/organization, 97–98
identifying lack of purpose, 26
identifying supplier squeezing,
    58–59
jobs, exporting, 79–80
Joiner, Brian, 42

K

Kelleher, Herb, 29

L

layoffs, employee
  avoidance techniques, 64–68
  causes, 125
  companies avoiding, 2, 10, 44
  costs, 4–5, 63, 117
  as indicator of organizational decline, 2,
    6–7, 14, 43, 62–68, 82
  management bonuses and, 67–68
  outsourcing and, 79–80
  stock price, influence on, 15
leaders. *See also* managers
  bosses contrasted with, 10
  ego of, 9, 10
  personal involvement/passion, 24–25,
    124–125
  responsibilities, 10, 31–32, 44, 64,
    117–118, 127
lean manufacturing, 6
losses, heavy, 30, 161–162
lost focus, defined, 162. *See also* purpose,
    organizational
lost tools/equipment, 92–93

M

M. D. Anderson Cancer Center, 19, 20
machine/equipment problems, detecting,
    93–94
maintenance, preventive, 5, 8, 85–90
management styles
  atomistic, 99
  crisis-mode, 4, 161
managers. *See also* leaders
  characteristics of, 71
  development, 23, 75–78, 81. *See also*
    development, employee

fear, 9
  knowledge, lack of, 9
  maintenance, attitude toward, 86–87, 90
  performance evaluations, view of, 71
  purpose, communication of
    organizational, 18
  transferring, 77–78
manufacturing companies
  layoffs, 63
  organizational decline, 4
  work environment, 90–91. *See also*
    work environments,
    dirty/disorganized
manufacturing, lean, 6
market capitalization, 12
mergers, 21–23
metrics, business, 30–31
mission. *See* purpose, organizational
mission statements, 18–21
mistakes, learning from, 128
money as sole organizational purpose, 26
money machines, companies as, 15
motivation, employee, 2–3, 17–18, 19. *See*
    also performance evaluations
Motorola, 32
music media, 24, 25

N

The New Economics (Deming), 50, 113
Nissan Corporation, 51
Nucor Steel, 2, 10, 44, 61
number obsession. *See* financial
    indicators, focus on

O

objective, project, 151
online bidding for supplies, 54–55
organization, defined, 11
organizational decline
  hidden, 1–4
  overview, 1–2
  reversing, 5–10
  stages, 2, 5
  warning signs. *See* warning signs
out-of-control systems, 36, 38
outsourcing, 79–80

P

parent poisoning, 21, 22–23, 162
Part Characteristics Matrix, 155, 156

passion, leader, 24–25
pay cuts, 43
PDSA (Plan-Do-Study-Act)
  benefits, 104–105
  example, 106–109
  overview, 10, 102–104
  process, 105–106, 129
performance evaluations
  changes in, 137
  costs, 70, 71
  eliminating, 74
  examples, 68–70
  intended benefits, 73, 80–81
  justification for use, 72–73
  legal issues, 72
  limitations, 76, 118
  management view of, 71
  poor performers and, 71–72
  statistical comparison, 74–75
  360° feedback process, 73–74, 81
performance, factors affecting worker, 119
performance improvements, reasons for
    failure, 6, 66
Perkins, Gene, 67, 97
personal involvement, leaders', 24–25,
    124–125
physical assets, maintenance of, 5, 8,
    85–90
Plan-Do-Study-Act (PDSA). *See* PDSA
planning, strategic, 133
policies as indicator of undervaluing
    employees, 81–82
Porras, Jerry, 13
Process Characteristics Matrix, 155, 156
Process Control Matrix, 155, 156
products
  assessing competitive position, 152
  company purpose and, 23–24
  customer satisfaction and, 23–24
  development deadlines, 100
  variation within, 47
profit centers, 16–17, 120–121
profits, role of, 13–16
promote or fire policy, 81
promotion from within, 23, 75–78, 81
psychology, lack of knowledge about, 9,
    10
purchasing, 52–53, 54–55, 100. *See also*
    suppliers
purpose, organizational
  assessing, 20, 133

Index **169**

benefits, 11–12, 14, 16, 21
  defined, 11, 162
  identifying lack of, 26–27
  management communication of, 18
  mergers/acquisitions and, 21–23
  product and, 23–24
  statements of, 18–21

Q

quality, 5, 94
Quality Function Deployment (QFD), 120,
  151–156, 162

R

reductions in force (RIF). *See* layoffs,
  employee
reflection, operational, 128–132, 157–159.
  See also PDSA
RIF (reductions in force). *See* layoffs,
  employee
RyanAir, 44, 61

S

safety, workplace, 92
sales, 101, 114–117
Scripps College, 19, 20
Scripps, Ellen Browning, 20
Senge, Peter, 50
service companies
  layoffs in, 63
  organizational decline in, 4
  preventive maintenance in, 88.
    See also maintenance, preventive
  work environment, 91–92
shareholders. *See* investors
Shewhart, Walter, 102, 145
shipping goals, monthly, 100–101
Six Sigma, 6, 103
Southwest Airlines
  employees, company view of, 61
  lack of layoffs, 10, 44, 65
  leadership, 8
  market capitalization, 12–13
  planning process, 29
  purpose, 25–26, 32
SPC (statistical process control). *See*
  statistical process control
spreadsheets, 30
stable systems, 36–37, 145, 147,
  162

statistical process control (SPC)
  benefits, 35–37
  defined, 162
  examples, 36–41
  method, 145–149
  requirements for, 41–42
  resources for learning about, 42
  status quo treatment of acquired company,
    21, 22
stocks, 14–15. *See also* investors
strategic planning, 133
subsidiary dilution, 21, 22
supplier squeezing. *See also* suppliers;
  total cost
  costs, 4, 45, 57
  defined, 162
  delaying payments to, 52, 53
  identifying, 58–60
  online bidding, 54–55
suppliers. *See also* supplier squeezing
  continual improvement, 56–57
  contributions of, 51
  costs associated with, 49
  development, 57–58, 121
  motivation, 8
  reducing number, 55–56
  selecting, 56
  surveying, 58
  turnover, 49–55, 162
support, technical, 14
surveys, supplier, 58
systems, stable/unstable, 36–38, 145, 147,
  162
systems thinking, 50, 51, 112–113, 117,
  163. *See also* fragmentation,
  departmental

T

target values, product, 153
teamwork, lack of, 30, 76–77,
  109–112
technical support, 14
360° feedback process, 73–74, 81
total cost, 45–49, 50–51, 55, 163
Toyota Motor Company
  company view of employees, 61, 64
  employee view of company, 135
  growth strategy, 23
  lack of layoffs, 10, 44
  leadership, 8
  market capitalization, 12–13

170 *Index*

production system, 33, 64
purpose, 26, 32
The Toyota Production System: Beyond Large-Scale Production (Ohno), 64
training, employee, 14, 23, 75–78, 81
transformation, business
  action plan, 132–134, 137–138
  culture and, 126
  defined, 123–124, 161
  fear of, 9
  fun environment, creating, 135
  leaders, personal involvement of, 24–25, 124–125
  leadership, changes in, 77–78
  ongoing nature of, 128
  reasons for lack of, 9–10
  reflecting on, 128–129, 132, 157–159. *See also* Five Whys; PDSA
  requirements, 125–128, 135
  timing, 126
transformation, personal, 128

U

Understanding Statistical Process Control (Wheeler), 42
undervaluing employees. *See also* layoffs, employee; performance evaluations
  costs, 63, 78–80
  defined, 61, 163
  history, 61–62
  identifying, 2, 8, 80–83
unstable systems, 36, 38

V

vision, defined, 11, 163

W

warning signs
  assessment, 132–133, 137–144
  defined, 163
  recognizing, 6–8. *See also* financial indicators, focus on; fragmentation, departmental; purpose, organizational; supplier squeezing; undervaluing employees; work environments, dirty/disorganized
Washington Post, 42
Western Electric Rules (Small), 147–149
Wheeler, Donald, 42
work environments, dirty/disorganized
  benefits of eliminating, 92–94
  costs, 86–87, 88, 91–94
  defined, 161
  5S method for improving, 94–97, 161
  identifying, 97–98
  as symptom of decline, 8, 85
  view of in business environment, 90–93
work environments, productive, 92, 135
workforce reductions. *See* layoffs, employee